Dear Believer

by
Allious Gee

Copyright © 2018 by Allious Gee
Published by Allious Gee
Durham, NC

All rights reserved. No part of this publication may be reproduced, distributed, or transmitted in any form or by any means, including photocopying, recording, or other electronic or mechanical methods, without the prior written permission of the publisher, except in the case of brief quotations embodied in critical reviews and certain other noncommercial uses permitted by copyright law.

Editors: Whitney Bennett – Bennett Creative |
    Cherie Graham –Start Write, LLC
Layout Design: Erica Smith
Front Cover Design: James Bennett – Bennett Creative
Back Cover Design & Book Project Management:
    Rainah Davis –Start Write, LLC

ISBN-13: 978-0-9994626-1-4

Dedication

This book is dedicated to the members of Faith Fellowship Ministries of Long Island, New York. Though you were small in number, there was nothing small about your love, dedication, and determination to persevere and live right. Serving as your minister humbled me, affirmed me, blessed me and taught me many valuable lessons on leading God's precious people. I am honored to have been a part of such a distinguished group of believers.

Contents

Author's Note	1
Supernatural Increase	2
All Power	4
Raised Up and Seated	6
A New Level	8
Build Your Faith Now	10
Why is God Allowing This?	12
Your Anointing	14
Exercise Dominion	16
The Greater/Stronger One	18
Unbeatable	20
Your Father's Words	22
Faith Is Work	24
Necessary Conflicts	26
Praying With Confidence	28
Full Joy	30
The Remedy for Fainting	32
Meet the Conditions	34
Jesus Recovered All	36
Keep Up the Faith Pressure	38
Receive Everything!	40
Missing Ingredients	42
Receiving	44
You Will Receive	46
The God Who Gives Good Things	48
Prayer Insights	50
Temporary Obstructions	52
Effective Praying	53
You Will Have What You Say	56
Don't Settle for Less	57
Pull Down Hopelessness	59

Time To Reign	61
Shame On You	63
Ministry In India	65
Your Authority as a Believer	68
Words That Change Your Future	70
Your Heart Your Mouth	72
Words That Move God	74
The Power of Your Words	77
You Can Have What You Say	79
Right Standing With God	81
Right From the Beginning	83
What Happens When We Sin?	85
The Integrity of Words	87
Have the God Kind of Faith	89
The Process	91
The Road to the Miraculous	93
The Enemy in My Thoughts	96
Winning Is Our Family Tradition	98
Take Time and Meditate	100
Prepare For the Glory	102
Wisdom for Long Trials	104
Walk By Faith Not By Sight	106
Believing To See	108
Competing for High Stakes	110
Lord, What's Taking So Long?	112
What's The Hold Up?	115
Waiting in His Presence	117
A Certain Amount	119
Spending the Time Required	121
Using the Little You've Got	123
Use Whatever God Provided	125
God's Way	127
Seeds	129
Keep Watch Over Your Words	131
The Manifestation Process	133

Almost Too Good To Be True ... 135
Faith Beyond Hopelessness ... 137
Faith That Makes God Take Notice ... 140
Sowing In Tears Reaping In Joy ... 142
I Will Never Leave You Nor Forsake You ... 144
Let's Praise and Worship the Lord ... 146
Words That Come To Pass ... 149
Living on a Higher Level ... 151
Faith That Grows Stronger With Time ... 154
Faith Never Grows Old ... 157
Basics for Strong Faith ... 160
Your Faith is Waiting to Serve You ... 162
Top Ten Reasons to Believe ... 164
Remember What He Said to You ... 167
Blessed With Every Spiritual Blessing ... 169
Everyone who Asks Receives (Matt. 7:8) ... 171
Receiving is Automatic ... 173
Advanced Provisions ... 175
Rising Above the Clouds ... 177
Reconciled ... 179
Disarm the Enemy ... 181
It's Your Unbelief! ... 183
Impossible ... 185
The Greatest Proof of All ... 187
Don't Take "No" for an Answer ... 189
Who Can I Count On? ... 191
Temporary Setbacks ... 193
Fire the Big Guns ... 195
Just Keep Going ... 197
"Lord, Make Him Pay" ... 199
Conceive the Image ... 201
It's Not What It Appears to Be ... 203
Look Through the Eyes of God ... 205
Jesus Recovered All ... 207

Author's Note:

Dear Believer,

I recently had someone send me messages by email. I thought like some of you, after having so many messages on my email, that this was another irritating and useless waste of my precious time. I forced myself to read it because it came from a friend. Little did I know that because I was so rushed and hard to reach, this was God's loving way of getting much needed spiritual healing and nourishment to me. After all, if He fed Elijah by the ravens, He could send my spiritual sustenance by email. After that, I always took the time to read what the Lord sent.

I decided to attempt to give that same type of encouragement to others through the same medium. The following are selected short readings that will build your faith and strengthen your resolve to trust God in the difficult seasons. Each is a word from the Lord for you.

Be Blessed
Al

Supernatural Increase

Dear Believer,

Any serious gardener or farmer treats the seed he or she is planting very carefully. The harvest will directly affect their quality of life. In the gardener's case, the row of seed is labeled because the gardener knows once it's in the ground it's very possible to forget what was planted. When you don't remember what was planted, how can you properly care for the seed?

It is God who gives us the power to get wealth (Deuteronomy 8:18). The ability and opportunity to sow and reap is that power. I do believe that the concept of sowing and reaping is so simple; it's easy to underestimate the power of it. Coupled with the sporadic results and financial lack we have all experienced, there is a temptation to disregard the whole thing. But we cannot judge the power of God's principles by our past experiences. Let's get a fresh revelation of this principle and find out where we've missed it. I know that the enemy has spent a lot of time making sure we are both confused and frustrated when it comes to sowing and reaping, but from what I've been able to study, there is supernatural increase waiting for the individuals who walk in this truth.

These days we're going to need the God-kind of wealth to do what we need to be done in ministry. The devil can defeat any natural attempt. But he is defeated by the action of faith (1 John 5:4). Most people are trying to hold on tightly to any income they have. However, in the kingdom, we are instructed that it is more blessed to plant finances into good ground and believe God for a supernatural increase. Let's follow the principles of the kingdom and expect the supernatural response from the Lord. He's the one who promised to pour out a blessing that there would not be room enough to receive (Malachi 3:10).

All Power

Dear Believer,

Jesus said in Matthew 28:18, "All power is given unto me in heaven and in earth" (King James Version). When God makes a statement like this, very few people are surprised. After all, He is God, and we expect Him to be all powerful. But we must also remember that Jesus was the son of Mary and very much a man. For this statement to be uttered by a man was something quite unique. No man before this could ever seriously make such a claim. But after conquering our ancient enemy, death, Jesus declared to all mankind that a new reality had been born. How thrilling this is to consider! It's even more thrilling as we begin to line our faith up to exercise it.

Surprisingly, what Jesus did not say is just as important. He did not say, "Now that I've got all power I'm going to take charge and be the supreme ruler over the earth." After such a thorough and complete defeat of His enemies, dominion was His for the taking. Who in the universe could stand in His way? Instead, He shifted the power to you and me.

He said, "You go into all the world and preach the gospel. From this point on I'll be with you." Essentially, He shared the "all power" experience with anyone who would believe. He said that the signs of this "all power" experience would manifest by the healing of the sick, protection from deadly things, casting out devils, and speaking with new tongues.

We must realize that everything Jesus owns also belongs to every believer. The scripture declares, "As he is, so are we in this world" (1 John 4:17). That would mean that we as believers are also destined to experience "all authority." Some faithful Christians get worried when we talk about believers having such power. However, there is a balance. This only works by love; just as Jesus gave His life completely as an expression of His love for the world and therefore experienced all power. We also will only experience this great power as we walk in His love.

Raised Up and Seated

Dear Believer,

> "For my thoughts are not your thoughts, neither are your ways my ways, saith the Lord. For as the heavens are higher than the earth, so are my ways higher than your ways, and my thoughts, than your thoughts."
>
> (Isaiah 55:8,9)

For years, we viewed this scripture as proof of a gulf permanently fixed between God and man. How could we ever be expected to know about the things of God or get close to him with such a wide gap? We all resigned ourselves to the unchangeable reality that He's God, we're mortal men, and never the twain shall meet. Right? After all, who could ascend such a distance from earth to heaven? I have heard so many read this verse and become complacent in the thinking that, "we can never know what God's going to do."

I went along with this misconception until I read Ephesians 2:6. It states, "And hath raised us up together and made us sit together in heavenly places." According to the Word of the Lord, we have been raised and elevated by the Lord himself into the heavenly realm. That would mean that the great and vast distance that separated us from God is now no more. We should no longer allow any separation. That's a new level of existence for us. We must begin to recognize this as an exciting fact.

A New Level

Dear Believer,

We must understand that since we are in the kingdom of God, we are now at a new level. This new level of knowledge, called revelation knowledge is not limited to the sense knowledge in which we were trained from our childhood to the present. But knowledge we get from "downloading" from the Holy Spirit. In this way, we actually begin to access God's thoughts and God's mind (1 Corinthians 2:10-16). To access such thoughts day and night transform us more and more into His likeness . We actually are taking on "divine nature" (2 Peter 1:3-4). How can we think His thoughts and meditate on His concepts and not be totally changed? His thoughts are illumination from heaven teaching us how to walk in total authority on earth. Years ago, I heard Kenneth Hagin say, "It's thinking faith thoughts and speaking faith words that bring the soul out of defeat into victory." What a level of abundant life we have been blessed by God to experience.

Meditating (muttering, memorizing, repeating, pondering. etc.) the Word of God and praying in tongues increases the flow of revelation knowledge to us. Revelation knowledge is what I believe the Lord wants us to walk in continuously. Can you imagine the effect on your life from continually walking in revelation knowledge!? "Get ready! Get ready! Get ready! Get ready!" In Deuteronomy 28:13, He states, "And thou shalt be above only." This is a new level for us who have for so long known only the opposite.

This is so wonderful! Not only new knowledge but a new level of peace, prosperity, love, health, and on and on, is ours in the kingdom of God. Please claim your place on this new level. We are His sons and daughters and we are in the ruling family. God is our dad. Be raised up and seated in the heavenly realm as His Word says.

Build Your Faith Now

Dear Believer,

The scripture declares, "This is the victory that overcomes the world even our faith" (1 John 5:4). Our faith determines what happens. Jesus said to the woman with the issue of blood, "Thy faith hath made the whole" (Mark 5:34). That's why it's important to diligently build up your faith. This is done by feeding on God's Word. Faith comes "by hearing, and hearing by the word of God" (Romans 10:17). Even when you think nothing is happening, feed your faith the Word of God. Build your faith muscles so that when you have to face a heavyweight problem the strength will be there.

So many people relax after their trial has subsided and things are going better. But don't be deceived, we should always be sober and vigilant (1 Peter 5:8). Although I haven't yet seen the kind of miracles I desire to experience, I continue to build my faith capacity. We don't always know when we'll need to use our faith, but we can prepare ourselves for it now. It's terrible when tragedy hits and people only have knowledge of the natural realm with its limitations. They have to learn faith in the midst of the storm because a miracle requires faith. It is sometimes very difficult to take the stand of faith in those times, but it can be done. How much better it is to learn while we are at relative peace? How blessed we are to know that even if our faith is as small as a mustard seed we can move mountains and "nothing shall be impossible unto you" (Matthew 17:20).

Some time ago, in the middle of the night I received a call; the kind every parent of a young adult male dreads. My son had been arrested and was being charged with possession of drugs. Because I was living in North Carolina and, at the time, he was in New York, there was little I could do.

My wife and I prayed and believed God that he would be safe in jail and that things would turn out alright. We stood on God's Word as the proceedings were drawn out over a year. In short, the Lord undertook our cause. The arresting officer was relieved of duty and the charges thrown out. My son learned the kind of lesson he will never forget, and God delivered him with no harm to himself and no blemish on his record.

Praises to our God.

Why is God Allowing This?

Dear Believer,

A couple days ago as soon as I woke up, the Holy Spirit began to communicate a thought to me. "Why," He asked (not because He didn't know the answer, but He wanted me to search deeper). "Why didn't God do anything about Goliath on behalf of the Israelites during the time of King Saul?" Centuries earlier, He defeated the great Pharaoh and the whole Egyptian army. Why didn't God do anything directly to stop the Philistines and Goliath from their invasion into the territory of his people? Goliath was a monster, towering over the people, cursing the Israelites. Saul and his army were stopped in their tracks at the very sight of this super-sized nightmare. Fear froze them in place. But surprisingly, God didn't move to hurt the Philistines or their champion. One might even conclude that if one bold shepherd boy hadn't come along when he did, things might have turned disastrous for Israel. Didn't God know the potential for disaster here?

You may be wondering the same thing right now about a fearsome giant you're facing. Debt, sickness, discouragement are all giant problems. *"Doesn't God know about this problem? Why is he allowing this to confront me without making some effort to remove it? Why isn't God doing something about this?"* We must learn that there are some things God can't do for us. Not because He doesn't have the ability. He has more than enough. But once He equips His people with His Word and His promises, the authority is then transferred to them.

We may have missed the transfer that occurred when Jesus said, "Whatever you bind on earth I'll bind in heaven and whatever you loose on earth I'll loose in heaven" (Matthew 18:18). He also said, "Whatever you ask...that will I do" (John 14:13). If we don't use what He has given us against the enemy, He cannot intervene. He would have to violate His own Word to come back into the situation and take over. When God promises to bind what we bind and to do whatever we ask Him, the next move is ours.

Your Anointing

"You have an anointing."
(1 John 2:20 New International Version)

Dear Believer,

I'm impressed of the Lord to remind and inform you today of what you have already received from the Lord. The scripture above actually reads, "You have an unction from the Holy One." This is something given to us from the Holy One, the Lord Himself. Anointing was always something special. Oil was poured or smeared upon an individual's head to signify the presence of God for rule or special assignment. In the Old Testament, both kings and priests were anointed to signify that, before God, they had a special appointment.

The same is true for you. You have a special appointment before the Lord. Anointed people are marked people. You may sometimes feel like you're marked for hard times or trouble because of the way things have transpired in your life, but it's not all bad. To be marked for the attack of the enemy is also to be marked for unusual victories and conquests.

If recognized and nurtured, the anointing absolutely transforms us. It totally changes our walk with God and emboldens us for His work. The same disciples who ran when Jesus was being crucified became courageous and bold when anointed by the Holy Ghost. His anointing is upon you to do the same thing.

Satan always shows up with one mission, to kill, steal and destroy (John 10:10 King James Version). The only reason God would let him near you is to exercise your newly found power. When the disciples came to Jesus having failed to cast out a lunatic spirit, Jesus informed them that even a small amount of what they had received was able to move mountains (Matthew 17:20).

Anointing, as defined by Isaiah 10:27, is the burden lifting, yoke destroying power of God. Burdens are lifted and yokes are absolutely destroyed because of it. It's powerful stuff! Today, let's first take time and recognize the fact that we have "an anointing" that sets us apart. Think on this thought today, *"I am anointed by God. God has poured upon me the power to lift burdens and destroy yokes."*

Exercise Dominion

Dear Believer,

I know that many of us are yet searching to know our "life assignment" from the Lord. We may have some inclination toward certain aspects of ministry, but nothing really clear. We know that the scripture states, "And we know that all things work together for good to them that love God, to them <u>who are the called according to his purpose</u> (Romans 8:28). This makes it so important to be operating in the purpose God has assigned us. That's where God's provision and His protection reside. Then we have assurance that "all things will work together for our good." But finding your true purpose can take time and seasons of prayer before the Lord. It is a process of discovery to learn of your divine mission. What happens to my life in the meantime? Am I in line for defeat for not being certain? Most certainly not!

When we are uncertain of our specific assignment, we can rest in God's original design for man. He said, "Let us make man in our image…and let them have dominion" (Genesis 1:26). Don't allow the devil any room to interfere during your discovery season. You have the God-given, God-designed and God-ordained right to exercise "dominion." It was yours from the beginning. Adam lost it, but Jesus got it back. Look throughout the scriptures. You will see that God supports those who will submit to His Word and will **take dominion**. You might not understand everything there is to your authority in this world, but that's not necessary. We don't all have the knowledge to build a car, but we have the keys to drive one.

Be bold! God is with you. Take your authority today in the name of Jesus!

The Greater/Stronger One

Dear Believer,

In 1 John 4:4, the scripture states, "Ye are of God, little children, and have overcome them,: because greater is he that is in you, than he that is in the world." Even though God calls us "little children," He informs us that we are of God, and the person we have resident within is greater than our enemy in the world. The Holy Spirit that we possess is the greater One, much stronger and more intelligent than any foe we face and He lives on the inside of us. We don't have to fear.

I like what Jesus said in Luke 11:21-22 (Living Bible), "For when Satan, strong and fully armed, guards his palace, it is safe—until someone stronger and better armed attacks and overcomes him and strips him of his weapons and carries off his belongings." Jesus said that even the gates of hell shall not prevail against us (Matthew 16:18). We have authority to break through those gates and take back our stolen goods with interest. Use the Word of God today and the name of Jesus and recover your stolen goods.

James 4:7 states, "Submit yourselves therefore to God. Resist the devil, and he will flee from you." When we submit to the plan and will of God for our lives, our confrontations with the enemy always end in him ultimately running away. No one enjoys the beating and bruising that comes from the violent attack of a much stronger individual. Imagine being attacked by God. Don't be fooled by Satan's deceptions, he must run to keep from being destroyed.

Unbeatable

Dear Believer,

Do you know that you can trip and fall in your walk with God and still get the victory? Satan knows that about you too, and he can't do a thing about it. I'm not only speaking of falling into some fleshly sin. I'm speaking of trying to succeed, but falling hard on your face. Sometimes we need to be reminded that being knocked down is not the end of the fight. A true believer can be knocked down, <u>but not knocked out</u>. Imagine what that does to the mind of your opponent as you keep rising every time he thinks you're done. We can do this because God always uplifts us with the unseen force of his powerful hand. In Psalm 37:23-25, it is written, "The steps of a good man are ordered by the Lord: and he delighteth in his way. Though he fall he shall not be utterly cast down: for the Lord upholdeth him with his hand. I have been young, and now am old: yet have I not seen the righteous forsaken, nor his seed begging bread."

In the hours we face hard trials, we must know in our spirit that despite outward appearances the situation is never hopeless. Knowing this, we can face our zero hours as a moment of decision which calls for tenacity even when our knees wobble and shake. 1 John 5:4 states, "For whatsoever is born of God overcometh the world: and this is the victory that overcometh the world, even our faith." Benson Idahosa, a preacher of the gospel who changed the face of Africa with his powerful teachings and miraculous works, made a statement I had to share with you. He said, "The greatest bulwark of Christian hope in any area of endeavor, including ministry, is the absolute certainty of final victory, the unshakable knowledge that in all things we are more than conquerors through Christ (Romans 8:37). The full realization of this truth will turn you around full circle and open to you vistas of courage and indomitable faith through the power of the Son of God, enabling you to rise up out of the quagmire of depression and despair and soar to the heights of hope and joy where God wants you to live."

Your Father's Words

Dear Believer,

Do you love the Lord? If you do, there are personal promises directly from the Father that belong to you. They're found in Psalm 91. It begins, "He that dwells in the secret place of the most High." To rid ourselves of the spirit of fear, this is must reading. Its words are a daily source of strength.

Surprisingly, this chapter, which starts out with the voice of David, ends with the voice of God. As we read it, the voice of our Father God intervenes with divine promises in the last three verses. In verses 14-16 He says,

> "Because he has set his love upon me, therefore will I deliver him: I will set him on high, because he hath known my name. He shall call upon me, and I will answer him: I will be with him in trouble; I will deliver him, and honour him. With long life will I satisfy him, and shew him my salvation."

If you love the Lord, these promises are yours personally from your Father God. Meditate on these three verses today and see what the Lord says to your heart through them.

Faith Is Work

The people asked Jesus,

> **"What shall we do, that we might work the works of God? Jesus answered and said unto them, This is the work of God, that ye believe on him whom he hath sent."**
>
> (John 6:28-29)

Dear Believer,

The work of God assigned to us is to believe. It sounds so simple, but it's the ultimate work assignment, to believe. It's also the one area where we encounter subtle enemy attacks, loss of focus, troubling uncertainty and disturbing doubts. Whatever we allow, our faith will either be weakened from past faith failures and disappointments, or strengthened through patience and feeding on God's Word. This is the area the enemy knows must be won at all costs, or he and his whole army are finished.

Unfortunately some "believers" are not as serious about faith as their arch nemesis. While some Christians play games in the area of faith, Satan infects them with weaknesses that render faith ineffective. Fears and doubts are among the most prominent faith infirmities.

None of us can afford not to secure this area. Whatever it takes, build your faith. Here's a great statement, "Doubt your doubts and believe your beliefs, but never believe your doubts and never doubt your beliefs." Your faith will determine your quality of life in God. Although you may already be saved, your faith will be the difference between a defeated or a victorious life. Do yourself a big favor; strengthen your faith daily. Feed and meditate on the Word of God. (Psalm 1, Romans 10:17). Act like the Word is true (James 2:26). Your faith is designed to make you win. Remember 1 John 5:4, "and this is the victory that overcometh the world, even our faith."

Necessary Conflicts

"Thou preparest a table before me in the presence of mine enemies."

(Psalm 23:5)

Dear Believer,

Today, God has a table prepared for you right in the presence of your enemies. Don't be afraid to confront your enemy. When we pray for peace, we usually mean tranquility, the wonderful quietness that accompanies the end of struggle, or the calmness and serenity that goes with rest and leisure in a chosen vacation spot. Our goal and the goal of many nations in the world is to be at peace. We desire a world without war or conflict. Outwardly, everyone is seeking peace. Admittedly, peace is a great treasure, but we need to be careful here. Some of the things we desire to receive from God will not come without confrontation.

All my life I thought that peace was the main goal when dealing with people. I sought after it on every level. I felt badly if anyone was upset with me. But masquerading as peace, this was actually <u>a crippling need to be liked by</u>

people. Have you ever suffered from this ailment? It is borne out of fear of rejection. I've since learned that without confrontation there can be no victory. I'm not condoning strife, but I am saying we must exercise our authority. Active believers are aggressively moving in a direction that is on a collision course with the enemy.

Avoiding confrontation is not true peace. Just like Goliath, our enemy is emboldened when we avoid confronting him. For weeks, he was able to paralyze the Lord's people because no one wanted to confront him.

Likewise, there are times in our lives we just don't want to deal with unacceptable behaviors, habits or practices in those around us. But avoiding them will not make them go away. Confrontation is often unpleasant and conflict is undesirable, but both are unavoidable with Satan. However, on the other side of conflict there is a victory waiting. <u>But it is a victory you will never see if you avoid engaging your enemy.</u> As we resist the devil, he runs (James 4:7). He must, or he will be destroyed by the power of God. If you've been trying to fit in, <u>it's not going to work</u>. We are not called to peaceful coexistence. We are called to be the head and not the tail (Deuteronomy 28:13).

Praying With Confidence

"And be not conformed to this world: but be ye transformed by the renewing of your mind."

(Romans 12:2)

Dear Believer,

Paul is admonishing believers everywhere not to think like the world thinks. Many of the concepts we received from the world are just plain error, especially concepts about God. One of those concepts is the way we regard prayer. The world regards prayer as a largely religious experience with very little relevance to reality and little benefit except for the internal peace and tranquility it brings to the individual. But this is not the same emphasis the Word of God places on prayer.

Our prayer requests should be spoken with <u>faith</u> and <u>confidence</u>. Faith in God's almighty ability and confidence that He always hears us. Then we know we have our petition. Knowing we have our petition is critical.

> "And this is the confidence that we have in him, that, if we ask any thing according to his will, he hears us: And if we know that he hears us, whatsoever we ask, we know that we have the petitions that we desired of him."
>
> (1 John 5:14,15)

The uncertain pleadings that we have often brought before God as prayer very often lack the confidence spoken of here. James, the brother of Jesus, makes the point more emphatically. He states,

> "But let him ask in faith, nothing wavering. For he that wavereth is like a wave of the sea driven with the wind and tossed. <u>For let not that man think that he shall receive anything from the Lord.</u>"
>
> (James 1:6,7)

Pray with confidence. That's what God requires of you.

Full Joy

Dear Believer,

Jesus said, "Hitherto you have asked nothing in my name: ask, and ye shall receive, that your joy may be full" (John 16:24). This implies that asking is meant to be an exercise that, when answered, ultimately causes us to be full of joy. When have your prayers been answered so completely that you were full of joy? It appears that asking is designed to bring a level of joy that he calls "full." This isn't to be a one time experience. Each time we ask we are to receive and that will continue to result in our joy being full. It is apparent that the whole purpose for asking is to receive. That may be obvious but it implies total fulfillment. God plans for our asking to end in the fulfillment of all our requests. Jesus also said, "For every one that asketh receiveth" (Matthew 7:8).

Just think about that statement. Such a simple and forthright statement leaves us speechless. How can this be? Jesus didn't waver in speaking here. He said "everyone" and that is clearly what he meant. All of us who haven't experienced answers to prayers that we've prayed must now find out why. We all need to have our prayers answered to have full joy. Let's take the time necessary to find out what is hindering and remove it.

The Remedy for Fainting

"Also [Jesus] told them a parable, to the effect that they ought always to pray and not to "turn coward-faint, lose heart and give up."

(Luke 18:1 Amplified Bible, Classic Edition)

"Do not fret or have any anxiety about anything, but in every circumstance and in everything by prayer and petition [definite requests] with thanksgiving, continue to make your wants known to God."

(Philippians 4:6)

Dear Believer,

It is quite obvious when you read these passages that the place of prayer and the attitude of the Lord regarding it is much more important than we first imagined. Here, prayer is regarded as the remedy for "fainting and giving up." According to these scriptures, we aren't to worry or have any anxiety about <u>anything</u> because of the power and effectiveness of prayer. I'm sure you'll agree with me that these verses aren't referring to prayers that fail to receive answers from the Lord. Unanswered prayer leads to frustration and discouragement in our walk with God. It's time to put an end to this type of experience.

Praying the way the Lord prescribes for us to pray is designed to get answers <u>every time</u>. Jesus stated very forcefully in Mark 11:22-24 (King James Version) that speaking to mountains works every time you have faith in your heart toward God and in your words to change the situation. By that same principle, whenever we pray, we are to believe what we say is coming to pass, then we will have what we pray. Jesus said, "…believe that ye receive them and ye shall have them" (v. 24). If we don't include <u>believing we receive</u> in our prayer, sadly it won't be answered (see James 1:7). Let's practice this until we get it right, and start to experience daily answers to our requests and petitions. I feel that no matter how many times we fall short in this area, it's worth weathering the storm of adversity to get into the place with God where every prayer is answered.

Meet the Conditions

"If my people, who are called by my name, will humble themselves and pray and seek my face and turn from their wicked ways, then will I hear from heaven, and I will forgive their sin and will heal their land."

(1 Chronicles 7:14 New International Version)

"And when you stand praying, if you hold anything against anyone, forgive him, so that your Father in heaven may forgive you your sins."

(Mark 11:25)

Dear Believer,

We have all known that prayer is contact with God. It's talking directly to him without any interference or middle man. We feel that we can talk to God about anything and everything and that's the way it should be. We should be able to communicate with our Father as intimately and as often as we like. I really believe that the Lord loves this interaction as much as we do.

But, when it comes to getting prayers answered, there are conditions that must be met. The same as with our natural parents. It's one thing to sit down and talk to them about our problems and about how much we love and appreciate them. It's quite another thing when asking for money or to get them to make a costly purchase for us. All of our parents were different, but in every family that I know, there is usually much more involved when it comes to things that cost money. There are usually conditions that are stated that must be followed. However, if we meet the conditions, we can rest assured of the outcome. Good parents love to see their children do the right thing.

Jesus Recovered All

Dear Believer,

It is disturbing to me that so long after the sacrifice of the son of God and the precious blood he shed, many are still not benefitting the way God designed. Jesus came to recover all that was lost in the fall of Adam. It is absurd that anyone should remain in the predicament Jesus died to remove from us. Did you know that Jesus recovered all? There is nothing he left undone. We must grasp that fact and allow our lives to be totally changed by it.

We know that Adam's fall brought sin, sickness, hopelessness, fear, death, and doubt. Jesus, on the other hand, brought healing, faith, eternal life, abundance, and power. We need to realize that what God performed in Jesus is much more powerful than what Satan did in Adam. It's time to refuse and reject what the devil is sending our way. Let's take hold of all the blessings that came from His sacrifice at Calvary. The cross and the resurrection was much more powerful than the fall. We are no longer under the curse but the blessing. Let the power of all that Jesus recovered permeate your life today.

Look at what Jesus said, "The thief comes only in order to steal and kill and destroy. I came that they may have and enjoy life, and have it in abundance (to the full, till it overflows)" (John 10:10 Amplified Bible, Classic Edition).

Keep Up the Faith Pressure

"Jesus answered and said unto them, Verily I say unto you, If ye have faith, and doubt not, ye shall not only do this which is done to the fig tree, but also if ye shall say unto this mountain, Be thou removed, and be thou cast into the sea; it shall be done. And all things, whatsoever ye shall ask in prayer, believing, ye shall receive."

(Matthew 21:21-22 Kings James Version)

"For every one that asketh receiveth; what man is there of you, whom if his son ask bread, will he give him a stone? Or if he ask a fish, will he give him a serpent? If ye then, being evil, know how to give good gifts unto your children, how much more shall your Father which is in heaven give good things to them that ask him?"

(Matthew 7:8-11)Dear Believer,

It is quite evident in these scriptures above that Jesus came to inform us that the Father in heaven wants us to have life in abundance. That cannot happen without our prayer needs being answered. But as in everything else promised by God, there is an enemy positioned against us to prevent us from receiving our rightful possessions. He is attempting to remain there, hoping we will give up the pursuit. It's just a matter of time. As you apply faith pressure, he will flee. Keep the pressure on with your words and actions.

Please don't lose heart. Know that the words of Jesus are not just truth, but spiritual law. The words of Jesus are laws that govern the realm of the spirit, which rules the physical world. These laws must be exercised and sometimes forcibly applied in order to work on our behalf. Man's curse has been hanging around in the earth since Adam sinned. Its many miseries come automatically, just like weeds. The blessings Jesus spoke of, on the other hand, must be deliberately declared and acted upon by every believer. Keep declaring the words of God and walking in line with what the Word says. Due season is here.

Receive Everything!

Dear Believer,

It's great being alive and in the plan of the Lord. Romans 8:28 states that "all things work together for good to them that love God, to them who are the called according to his purpose." Let's believe that all day today. I'm excited about what the Lord has planned and designed for our prayer life.

When Jesus cursed the fig tree he said,

> "Verily say unto you, If ye have faith, and doubt not, ye shall not only do this which is done to the fig tree, but also if ye shall say unto this mountain, Be thou removed, and be thou cast into the sea; it shall be done. **And all things, whatsoever ye shall ask in prayer, believing, ye shall receive.**"
>
> (Matthew 21:21,22)

Everything we pray and believe for, God has planned for us to receive. Everything! Now I know that sounds extreme, especially when we are often very concerned that we may be asking for something that God doesn't want us to have.

But think about it, Jesus had just used the power of His words to curse a tree. That in itself sounds a bit farfetched to us. But when we walk in the kingdom of God we can expect the unusual and the supernatural to become commonplace. Certainly if you really love the Lord, you don't want the things that God doesn't want you to have. Our prayer problems are not in what we're asking as much as in whether we are believing we actually are receiving.

Missing Ingredients

Dear Believer,

Jesus said, "Therefore I say unto you, What things soever ye desire, when ye pray, believe that ye receive them, and ye shall have them" (Mark 11:24).

We need to put more effort and more focus on believing that we receive. This is the area where the enemy is continually launching his attack of doubt and uncertainty. As a result, many have succumbed and capitulated, accepting less that what Jesus said is ours. With what's at stake here, we cannot afford to give in. Unless we believe that we receive what we asked, nothing will happen. We don't have a problem praying and asking God. The problem is that when we pray, confidence and "believing we receive" are missing. Let's deliberately take some quality time when we pray to release faith and confidence that our petition is granted. Please meditate on this scripture today:

> **"And this is the confidence that we have in him, that, if we ask any thing according to his will, he heareth**

us: And if we know that he hear us, <u>whatsoever we ask, we know that we have the petitions</u> that we desired of him."

(1 John 5:14,15)

Receiving

Dear Believer,

I believe that one way to really understand what prayer was actually designed to be is to listen to what Jesus says about it. Then we can say what He says and be confident that we have the correct impression. Jesus said,

> "Ask, and it shall be given you; seek, and ye shall find; knock, and it shall be opened unto you: For <u>everyone that asketh receiveth</u>; what man is there of you, whom if his son ask bread, will he give him a stone? Or if he ask a fish, will he give him a serpent? If ye then, being evil, know how to give good gifts unto your children, how much more shall your Father which is in heaven <u>give good things to them</u> that ask him?"
>
> (Matthew 7:7-11)

It is obvious here that our Father in heaven designed for us to receive the very things we ask for, not some cruel substitute. Yet some believers are convinced that the opposite is true. In the mind of Jesus, everyone asking is receiving. Praise God!

This is ammunition against the doubts the enemy fires at us daily. No matter what we're experiencing, to know what Jesus's will is anchors our souls. It also gives us holy resolve to pursue His will. We can be certain that we have His divine assistance whenever we are attempting anything in line with it.

You Will Receive

Dear Believer,

"Jesus replied, Truly I tell you, if you have faith and do not doubt, not only can you do what was done to the fig tree, but also you can say to this mountain, Go, throw yourself into the sea, and it will be done, If you believe, <u>you will receive</u> whatever you ask for in prayer."

(Matthew 21:20-22 New International Version)

"In that day you will no longer ask me anything. Very truly I tell you, my Father will give you whatever you ask in my name. Until now you have not asked for anything in my name. Ask and <u>you will receive</u>, and your joy will be complete."

(John 16:23,24)

"Again, truly I tell you that if two of you on earth agree about anything they ask for, <u>it will be done for them</u> by my Father in heaven. For where two or three gather in my name, there am I with them."

(Matthew 18:19-20)

We can all see what's in the mind of Jesus regarding prayer. He speaks convincingly that whatever is asked is received. I love to think about this because it's so certain. He was not just speaking some nice idea, He was speaking spiritual law, which works every time for anyone. No matter what your experience has been with prayer, isn't it great to know that the Father has designed it to work every time for everyone? Now it's just a matter of making the necessary adjustment in our faith and our actions to experience the results. We can start by saying what Jesus says until it becomes a part of our lives.

The God Who Gives Good Things

Dear Believer,

Concerning our requests in prayer Jesus said, "For everyone who asks receives," (Matthew 7:8). With little or no hesitation, Jesus makes a statement that sounds to the natural mind as if He either was out of touch with the reality or He wasn't really paying close attention to the harsh predicaments facing man. The statement was made as if there was no doubt about the outcome of every prayer. Although they respected Jesus, this must have been just another one of those "mystical" statements. Philosophers and prophets of their day were often known for such. But to make His point more personal and more real to their everyday experiences, He reminded them of the need we all feel to satisfy our children's requests. He said,

> "What man is there of you, whom if his son ask bread, will he give him a stone? Or if he ask a fish, will he give him a serpent? If ye then, being evil, know how to give good gifts unto your children, how

much more shall your Father which is in heaven give good things to them that ask him?"

(Matthew 7:8-11 King James Version)

With one statement, Jesus totally shocked the entire crowd. The Jews knew of a God who had a reputation for power and punishment, but they had never been introduced to the Father who would answer every request. This was indeed a revolutionary new concept, a God who desired to give good things to His children. The words of Jesus revealed spiritual laws that were in effect at that time. From that point on anyone could rely on this law to work on their behalf. Can you believe what He said?

Prayer Insights

Dear Believer,

At a strategic time in the scriptures, Jesus repeated a mind blowing claim. He said, "And all things, whatsoever ye shall ask in prayer, believing, ye shall receive" (Matthew 21:22). This statement assures every believer of what God thinks regarding the certainty of prayer. We can no longer take it as lightly as we have in the past. Jesus spent time explaining and demonstrating the power and certainty of something we have experienced too often as "hit and miss." But we can no longer allow that type of thinking in our daily lives. Jesus wanted us to realize that when God hears us, which means we are praying in line with His Word, we have it. You can now confidently declare, "If He hears me, I have what I asked."

Can you imagine that? If God just hears your prayer request, you have it! If that sounds a bit extreme, consider this scripture:

> "And this is the confidence that we have in him, that, if we ask **anything** according to his will, he heareth us: And if we know that he hear us, whatsoever we ask, we know that **we have the petitions** that we desired of him."
>
> (1 John 5:14,15)

We cannot allow our prayers to be uncertain when the Lord has planned so lovingly to answer whenever he hears us. No wonder Paul later declared not to worry about anything and pray about everything (Philippians 4:6).

Now take some time and read John 11:41,42 and listen to what the Lord reveals to you.

Temporary Obstructions

Dear Believer,

Have you heard the saying that one word from God can change your life forever? I believe that statement is so true. Here is a word from the Lord for you today:

> **"For our light affliction, which is but for a moment, worketh for us a far more exceeding and eternal weight of glory; While we look not at the things which are seen: for the things which are seen are temporal; but the things which are not seen are eternal."**
>
> (2 Corinthians 4:17-18)

The Spirit of the Lord whispered to my heart that if you can see it with your natural eyes, it is temporary and subject to change.

Effective Praying

Dear Believer,

It is obvious that we don't see things the same way God sees them. He said this in Isaiah 55:8, "For my thoughts are not your thoughts, neither are your ways my ways, saith the Lord." Not realizing it, many of us stop short at that scripture, knowing that we'll just never be like God. But there can be much loss in our lives from seeing things differently. I often refer to the statement I read long ago. It goes something like this, "If we don't see things the way God sees them we are deceived." Now we can all appreciate the fact that we're not God. We can't even begin to think we are, <u>but</u> that doesn't excuse us from lining up with His truth. Seeing things the way God sees them is critical to our victory and deliverance.

It's just that way when it comes to praying to get results. Jesus said, "What things soever ye desire when ye pray, believe that ye receive them, and ye shall have them" (Mark 11:24). Such a simple statement from the mouth of Jesus is one that has been largely ignored for decades. We have not, as a habit, looked upon prayer as an exercise which requires us to believe we receive **when we pray**. God is then obligated to bring it to pass. But the scriptures bear out that prayer is not to be a hopeful exercise but rather an act full of confidence.

James said, "But let him ask in faith **nothing wavering**. For he that wavereth is like a wave of the sea driven with the wind and tossed...let not that man think that he shall receive any thing of the Lord" (James 1:6,7). It's quite a shock to realize that many of our prayers will not be answered because we neglected this area. But take heart, we can make a change right now.

Decide right now not to waver, but to take a stand on the Word of God. Jesus, who is the Word of God, said, "everyone who asks receives" (Matthew 7:8 New International Version). This is a glimpse into the mind and design of God for what prayer was meant to be. Never was it meant to be merely an exercise in hoping, but confidence is to be in full activation when we pray. 1 John 5:14-15 (King James Version) states,

> **"And this is the confidence that we have in him, that, if we ask any thing according to his will, he heareth us: And if we know that he hear us, whatsoever we ask, we know that we have the petitions we desired of him."**

Say this, "If he hears me, I have the petition." What a wonderful and exciting right and privilege to have our prayers answered when He hears us. Jesus said, "Everyone who asks receives."

Keep meditating on these verses and lessons until this becomes second nature to you and until you get it way down in your spirit.

You Will Have What You Say

Dear Believer,

Is it true that you can have what you say? If that sounds farfetched or extreme, just remember that Jesus was the One who said it. He said,

> "For verily I say unto you, That whosoever shall say unto this mountain, Be thou removed, and be thou cast into the sea; and shall not doubt in his heart, but shall believe that those things which he saith shall come to pass; <u>he shall have whatsoever he saith</u>."
>
> (Mark 11:23)

"He shall have whatsoever he saith." That sounds like, "You can have what you say." The conditions here are spelled out. Don't doubt in your heart but believe what you say is coming to pass and you will have what you say.

Whoever will take the time and effort to meet these conditions is in line to receive this promise. Are you up to the challenge?

Don't Settle for Less

Dear Believer,

Did you know that prayer is designed for you to receive good things from God. According to the teachings of Jesus, we are to receive the very things we ask for, not something different. Prayer is designed by God to end in receiving and in full joy. Jesus said,

> "Ask and it will be given to you; seek and you will find; knock and the door will be opened to you. For everyone who asks receives; the one who seeks finds; and to the one who knocks, the door will be opened. Which of you, if your son asks for bread, will give him a stone? Or if he asks for a fish, will give him a snake? If you, then, though you are evil, know how to give good gifts to your children, how much more will your Father in heaven give good gifts to those who ask him."
>
> (Matthew 7:7-11 New International Version)

"Very truly I tell you, my Father will give you whatever you ask in my name. Until now you have not

asked for anything in my name. Ask and you will receive, and your joy will be complete."

(John 16:23,24)

According to Jesus, our Father is better than us at giving good gifts. Then, why is it that so many believers who pray and do not receive what they ask, settle for less than what they requested? When our prayers end in our receiving the equivalent of stones and snakes, we should know that this was not the work of our Father. At that point, we need to take some time and locate the problem. Our enemy loves to intercept the blessing and send us a disappointment instead. Don't accept it! If we have to battle even in our prayers, let's do it! Let's be willing and ready to fight in our prayers and in our thoughts as well. Jesus said, "Everyone who asks receives." We don't have to accept less. Please take some time and read Daniel 10:12- 14.

Pull Down Hopelessness

Dear Believer,

We have power given to us by God to destroy strongholds. What is a stronghold? The definition given by Ed Silvoso is very helpful here. He defines a *stronghold* as **a mindset, impregnated with <u>hopelessness</u> which causes an individual to accept as unchangeable that which he knows is contrary to the will of God**. Satan uses "hopelessness" as a major weapon against the people of God. You may have at times in your life experienced its debilitating effects. But don't give in because we have the authority over this weapon. Paul stated,

> **"For the weapons of our warfare are not carnal, but mighty through God to the pulling down of strong of strongholds. Casting down imaginations."**
>
> (2 Corinthians 10:4,5 King James Version)

The effect of hopelessness on any believer is devastating. If we lose hope, faith has no foundation. "Faith is the substance of things hoped for" (Hebrews 11:1). We don't have to allow it in our thinking, not even for a moment.

Remember what Jesus said, **"nothing shall be impossible unto you"** (Matthew 17:20).

Time To Reign

Dear Believer,

The case for our righteousness is made in a statement by Paul to the Romans. He said,

> **"For if because of one man's trespass (lapse, offense) death reigned through that one, much more surely will those who receive [God's] overflowing grace (unmerited favor) and the free gift of righteousness [putting them into right standing with Himself] reign as kings in life through the one Man Jesus Christ (the Messiah, the Anointed One)."**
>
> (Romans 5:17 Amplified Bible, Classic Edition)

To our utter surprise and delight, we are informed here of our God-designed right to "reign as kings in life." The reason is simple. He starts by saying, "If by one man's trespass death reigned." None of us has not been affected by the reign of death. Death's reign is characterized by every misery inflicted upon fallen mankind with its accompanying fear and dread. However, no matter how effectively death has ruled in this world, it came as a result of one man's willful <u>mistake</u>. But our right to reign is <u>not a mistake</u>. We have God's backing. It is by God's design that you and I receive an abundance of His special favor. (I like to call us His favorites.)

Secondly, we also are given the "gift" of righteousness, placing us in right standing with him. We can now come into His presence without any sense of guilt, shame or condemnation. With such blessings comes an immediate and inherent authority to "reign as kings." We are to reign as kings in this life. Submit your life to this revelation and begin to reign from this moment forth. Refuse to be denied. Only then can we fulfill our role in Jesus being known as the King of Kings.

Shame On You

Dear Believer,

Guilt, condemnation and shame, are the weapons of our enemy, which are generated from our own consciousness. It is his delight to use our own thoughts against us accompanied by some form of each of these self-destructive forces. And, if you've ever been on the receiving end of this type of attack you know how timid and disheartened it can leave you.

Reliving past failures and blunders can cause us to live in a continual state of condemnation. We all fail and make mistakes. None of us is perfect.

But our adversary makes a point of showcasing all of our shortcomings to the point of utter humiliation. How often, at a moment's notice, he flashes a past indiscretion or sinful act across our minds. He is well known as The Accuser of the Brethren (Revelation 12:10). He loves nothing more than to subject us to unrelenting blame and ridicule from our own consciences. We can blame ourselves for so many things, and rightfully so. But take heart, God has the cure.

It's righteousness. That's right, righteousness! Righteousness, which is defined as being able to stand before God without any sense of guilt, shame or condemnation, is not earned, but bestowed as a gift. Paul said,

> **"They which receive abundance of grace and of the <u>gift of righteousness</u> shall reign in life by one, Jesus Christ."**
>
> (Romans 5:17 King James Version)
>
> **"For he hath made him to be sin for us, who knew no sin: that we might be made the righteousness of God in him."**
>
> (2 Corinthians 5:21)

At Calvary, there was a great exchange. Jesus became our sin and we became the righteousness of God. We are made the actual righteousness of God. It is our gift from the Lord. Can you believe this? Then, let's walk in the light of it.

Please read the entire fifth chapter of Romans (Amplified Translation if you have it).

Ministry In India

Dear Believer,

Did you ever wonder how God orchestrates the start of ministry into other countries? I'm going to relate a story to you that was told during our trip to the Dominican Republic. It shows the amazing ability of God to bring about His will for ministry in foreign lands.

On Saturday at noon, the ministry group was invited to a meeting of church leaders in the home of the pastor. When we arrived, the group was singing and worshipping the Lord. As each person sat around our group leader, Joseph, related a story that was so out of the ordinary it had to be God. He said he had a dream about being a passenger on a plane that was just about to land. On the plane, he could hear the flight attendant say over the speaker, "Please bring your seat backs to their upright position and secure your tray tables. Welcome to India." He said he could see through the window the plane flying low over the tops of the trees and landing. In the dream, after landing, he was ushered to a compound of buildings surrounded by a wall.

In the wall was a large hole, and children were peering from inside the walled area with their eyes fixed on him. He could hear them say as the eyes seemed to multiply, "Come over here and help us." Suddenly, behind him appeared a Sikh (a religious man dressed in a turban and traditional garb). This man smiled and his mouth was filled with gold. At that point, he said he woke up out of his sleep and sat up straight in bed. To him the dream was so real and so peculiar, it stayed on his mind.

While ministering in church, he was led to tell his dream. Upon telling it a woman came up to the front with tears streaming down her face. She said, I know what you dreamed about. As it turned out, this woman was the grand daughter of a great Christian apostle to India who had planted scores of churches in his lifetime. She told him that her father, the son of the apostle, was operating an orphanage in India, which was in need of help. As he laid hands on her to pray the Lord showed him the word "medicine." When asked about medicine, she stated that both she and her sister were doctors. Now, what she wanted most was to serve the Lord. The Sikh he saw in the dream, she told him, was a dentist of the Sikh religion who had volunteered to help them financially with the orphanage. She also had a brother who was studying medicine, who had rebelled against the family and the Lord. At that point a word of knowledge was given that their brother who had left would soon be restored back to his father.

After leaving that service, Joseph received an urgent call. They had just received the devastating news that the son, who had left the Lord had been murdered. He had just completed his medical studies and was robbed at gunpoint and fatally shot. Needless to say, this news was more than a little unsettling. But to Joseph's surprise, the father, who by now had been informed of his dream, contacted him pleading with him to come to Colorado to conduct the funeral. He consented and upon his arrival tried to comfort the family and friends with as much compassion as he could muster. He secretly wondered about the word he had given about the son returning to his father. This occasion would have been totally unbearable except for one revelation. The murdered son's roommate told the family that approximately 21 days before completing his studies, the son had given his life to God and was gloriously saved.

As a result of what began as a peculiar dream, an invitation was extended to Joseph and our ministry team to come to India and minister to leaders in government, businesses and churches. The invitation was accepted and the first trip was taken this past January. This was just the beginning. I met the owner of the orphanage at a recent meeting and was also given a cordial invitation to "Come to India." God is opening doors.

Your Authority as a Believer

Dear Believer,

Jesus made two statements regarding power in the Bible that are worth further study. He said,

> "Behold, I give unto you power to tread on serpents and scorpions, and over all the power of the enemy: and nothing shall by any means hurt you."
>
> (Luke 10:19)

> "Ye shall receive power, after that the Holy Ghost is come upon you."
>
> (Acts 1:8)

Both these statements speak of a wonderful transference of power to the believer. Both are mighty endowments given to the believer by God. Without them, we would have no real rule over the enemy in the earth. But each is different from the other.

The first statement on power in Luke is speaking of "authority" or as some people call it "delegated power."

This kind of power is only as strong as what is backing it up. For the believer, it's God. The full backing of God is behind this authority. It's very interesting to examine the God designed system set up to fortify every believer in the Lord Jesus Christ. Accordingly, Paul made a bold declaration in Romans 8:28-31. He said,

> **"And we know that all things work together for good to them that love God, to them who are the called according to his purpose. For whom he did foreknow, he also did predestinate to be conformed to the image of his Son, that he might be the firstborn among many brethren. Moreover whom he did predestinate, them he also called: and whom he called, them he also justified: and whom he justified, them he also glorified."**

God is the one who initiated all of the above. This describes the God- designed system backing up every believer. God is the one who has designed and constructed it so that **"all things work together for good"** for us. With such an elaborate fail-safe network behind us, Paul stated, **"What shall we say to these things? If God be for us, who can be against us?"** Please take some time and meditate on these scriptures. I believe God wants to speak to you regarding your authority in a more personal way.

Words That Change Your Future

Dear Believer,

Jesus said,

> "Whosoever shall say unto this mountain, Be thou removed, and be thou cast into the sea: and shall not doubt in his heart, but shall believe that those things which he saith shall come to pass; he shall have whatsoever he saith."
>
> (Mark 11:23)

Lately, I have again been urged to go back and refocus on this amazing principle. There are many important things that are done by speaking words but none of them is more important than the words spoken that ushered us into the kingdom of God. Each of us can remember when we made Jesus the Lord of our lives. At that moment, we obligated God to recreate our spirit man on the inside and pour into us His divine nature. And He did just that. What kind of words have the power to move God like that? Words that are believed in your heart and spoken out of your mouth (Romans 10:9). Jesus went on to say that when we pray, if we believe we receive what we pray for, we would have it. If we can speak words that alter our future and our ultimate destiny, what other powerful things can be done with our words?

I am a proponent of a consistent time of meditation on God's Word. The book of Joshua instructed him not to let God's words "depart out of thy mouth, but thou shalt meditate therein day and night...for then thou shalt make thy way prosperous" (Joshua 1:8). According to this verse, "we" have the power to make our way prosperous. When we meditate on the principle Jesus spoke of above, it appears that you can actually <u>have what you say</u>. This is not a principle that allows us to be reckless and irresponsible with our speech, but it is saying that faith words should be a routine part of our speech. That's exciting because the prospect of receiving based on our words opens up new avenues we've yet to explore. It means that our circumstances will respond to the words we say instead of our words responding to circumstances. I'm sure you've heard this before, but did you really get it?

Your Heart Your Mouth

Dear Believer,

Recently I returned to a revelation God gave to Paul in the book of Romans 10:6-10, it reads,

> "But the righteousness which is of faith speaketh on this wise, Say not in thine heart, Who shall ascend into heaven? (that is, to bring Christ down from above.) Or, Who shall descend into the deep? (that is, to bring Christ again from the dead.) But what saith it? The word is nigh thee, even in thy mouth, and in thy heart; that is, the word of faith, which we preach; That if thou shalt confess with thy mouth the Lord Jesus, and shalt believe in thine heart that God hath raised him from the dead, thou shalt be saved."

In this passage Paul makes a decree that is a drastic departure from the way believers have routinely done things. He first tells us what not to say. Don't say, "Who will go and bring Jesus down (to deliver us)?," nor should we say, "Who will go down and bring Jesus up from the dead (to deliver us)?" Over the years, we've all heard songs and prayers that plead with Jesus to "come by here." But Paul set out in this scripture to stop that type of praying once and for all time.

According to Paul, the power of deliverance from sin and other problems is no longer solely in the hands of God. He stated that this powerful word is now in **your heart** and in **your mouth**. The power to transform your life from a hell-bound slide to a heaven-bound rapture is now in your own mouth and your own heart. I think we can all agree that salvation is the single most important step of our lives. Nothing else is as important. And God has placed the power to accomplish that in our hands.

Believing and speaking is all that is required initially to cause this to be so. Until we believe and voice that belief nothing changes. But when we follow those simple instructions, critical changes occur immediately. This is not only a principle in salvation but also in everything we desire from the Lord. We must believe and say. According to Jesus, that's what causes it to be (Mark 11:22-24). Let's begin to practice this; only then can we perfect it.

Words That Move God

Dear Believer,

I am rediscovering the scriptural principle of confession. Paul stated,

> "For with the heart man believeth unto righteousness; and <u>with the mouth confession is made unto salvation.</u>"
>
> (Romans 10:10)

According to the revelation given to Paul by God, after believing with our hearts, the words we say with our mouths actually move God Almighty to immediately accept us into His kingdom. At the moment of our confession, we are transformed from a life that is replete with sin and ungodly actions into a world where we are squarely in God's favor. What a privilege and what powerful words! Entering the lifestyle and realm of salvation is no small thing. Before Jesus came, there was no road map to the kingdom of God. Paul here uncovers the mystery of just how we enter the kingdom. It's with a <u>believing heart</u> and <u>a confession</u>

or words. Some of us have lived the saved life for so long that we have a tendency to make light of its supernatural nature. Within the realm of salvation, we have the full rights and privileges of the very sons of God Himself. Paul opened up a revolutionary new concept to the church. But when you think about it, he was saying exactly what Jesus had decreed years earlier.

Jesus said,

> **"Have faith in God. Whosoever shall say unto this mountain, Be thou removed, and be thou cast into the sea; and shall not doubt in his heart, but shall believe that those things which he saith shall come to pass; he shall have whatsoever he saith."**
>
> (Mark 11:22,23)

When Jesus made this statement he had just demonstrated the power of this principle on a fig tree which he had cursed (Mark 11:14). He said this kingdom principle would work for whatever we say and for whosoever would do the saying. This challenges every believer to become effective in the things we say. Everything from our daily conversations to our words in prayer must now conform to this principle to be effective. A great faith teacher said there is a force much more powerful than the atomic bomb with its devastating radioactive fallout. It exists everywhere and it's the power of God. And this awesome power is accessed by our confession of faith. Don't miss or make light of the power of your words. Jesus spoke it. It is spiritual law.

We must confess healing while our bodies are yet feeling the effects of illness in order to bring the healing. We must confess prosperity while still suffering the effects of poverty. That's what changes the situation. The believing and speaking comes before the seeing and feeling. The enemy will fight us as he fought Jesus in Luke 4. He tried to sway him away from the mighty words that were both spoken and written. But Jesus would not be distracted. He said, "It is written," and "It is said" (Luke 4:12).

The Power of Your Words

Dear Believer,

The words of Jesus and others concerning the power of confession and the power of our words are truly amazing. Jesus said,

> "Whosoever shall say...He shall have whatsoever he saith."
>
> (Mark 11:23)
>
> "Ask, and it shall be given you. Every one that asketh receiveth."
>
> (Matthew 7:7,8)

Since we know that Jesus only spoke the words His Father gave Him to say, these statements are remarkable. It means that our Father God designed us to have all that we ask and all that we say when we believe. To have **_whatever_** you say and to receive what you ask is a blessing believers have not yet realized. Whatever your experiences with God, you must realize what is revealed in these verses. It is nothing less than God's extreme love for us being demonstrated.

He wants us to receive **everything**, **every time** we ask or say. That's powerful! To me, this is worth getting right no matter how much opposition we experience.

Paul wrote that this is not some elaborate process. He said simply that, **"The word is nigh thee, even in thy mouth, and in thy heart: that is, the word of faith, which we preach"** (Romans 10:8); In other words, by believing in your heart and speaking with your mouth, you have the power and authority to cause impossible things to come to pass. Think about that.

John stated,

> **"This is the confidence that we have in him, that, if we ask anything according to his will, he heareth us: And, if we know that he hear us, whatsoever we ask, we know that we have the petitions that we desired of him."**
>
> (1 John 5:14)

John says that we are confident of one thing—if he hears us we have what we asked (our petition). We have it! That's faith. Meditate on these verses and see what God is saying to you about them.

You Can Have What You Say

Dear Believer,

I continue to be astounded by the words of Jesus in Mark 11:22-23,

> "And Jesus answering saith unto them, Have faith in God.
>
> For verily I say unto you, That whosoever shall say unto this mountain, Be thou removed, and be thou cast into the sea; and shall not doubt in his heart, but shall believe that those things which he saith shall come to pass; he shall have <u>whatsoever he saith</u>."

For the many thousands of people who have felt powerless in this world, this statement is our deliverance. It's so simple. But it's a statement largely avoided by many Bible teachers and believers. Some even warn us not to take the Bible literally for fear of disappointment. Though well intended, I believe this is a clever disguise for doubt. Jesus promises that we can have what we say when we believe. I believe He meant what He said. So let's get in and stand on His promise. Just as the Israelites learned many things about God on the way to their promised land, you can be certain that we will learn much about God as we stand on His Word. But learning about God, even in the midst of trials, is a good thing.

Maybe there are some people who don't feel the need to rely upon God for their very survival, but I do. In my life, I must have something strong and certain to depend upon. This promise fits the bill. Is this easy? No! But it works. Over the years, I have had enough successes with this promise to know with all my heart that it works whenever exercised in faith. Every time I have faced alarming symptoms in my body, or desperate predicaments in my finances, and even sabotage by the enemy in my relationships, I knew that I could have what I said. And that is what persevered every time.

Right Standing With God

Dear Believer,

Of all the wonderful gifts that God gives, did you know that righteousness is one of them? Please take a look at Romans 5:17, "they which receive abundance of grace and of the gift of righteousness shall reign in life by one, Jesus Christ."

Righteousness means being able to stand in God's presence without any sense of guilt, condemnation or inferiority. This much sought after state, however, cannot be earned. So many have attempted but failed. To earn it would make it a reward for deeds done, trials endured or feats accomplished. Relatively few individuals would then be able to obtain it.

But, as the scripture states above, righteousness is a gift to all believers. Everyone loves to receive gifts, especially when they're unexpected and expensive. Righteousness fits both criteria. It was purchased with the precious blood of Jesus and is quite an unexpected blessing to all.

Also implied in the same verse is that it leads to "reigning in life." That's right, being right with God gives us the right to <u>rule on earth</u>. What is there about righteousness that would qualify us to reign or rule in this life? It is right standing with God, a right relationship between you and the head of the universe. Anyone who is right with God has already achieved the most sought after position there is in this life. What could be better? When we are right with God, we have divine favor qualifying us as "more than conquerors through him that loved us" (Romans 8:37). I am so thankful that we who are striving to make it to heaven don't have to wait to hear Jesus say, "Well done," to know that we are righteous. We have that gift now.

Right From the Beginning

Dear Believer,

As we consider our origin in this life, it is often said that we're "just sinners saved by grace." But it's time to make a permanent end to this thinking.

Our original state was not sin. Our natural state is righteousness. In other words, when we consider our true history, it's more natural for us to be righteous than sinner. Adam was born (created) righteous. He enjoyed a close relationship with God. After Adam's fall, every human being was born in sin and separated from God at birth.

Along with the fall came <u>guilt,</u> <u>shame</u> and <u>condemnation</u>. All were part of the curse. Jesus redeemed us from that curse when He sacrificed His life (Galatians 3:13). We are now once again being born into a close and privileged relationship with God. Let's get back to our natural state.

I have observed so many Christians who have accepted as fact that we were born into sin, but now fail to accept being born again righteous. They have not understood that to accept the gift of righteousness is to <u>return to our natural state</u>. Quite preoccupied with the failures and shortcomings of unrighteousness, they feel humble when they accept being a sinner saved by grace. This attitude does such disservice to the sacrifice of Jesus. It's time to completely throw off this thinking. If we accepted the sin birth, which resulted from Adam's wrong doing, we should much more willingly accept our natural righteous birth that resulted from Jesus doing right.

Make it part of your daily routine to say, "I am the righteousness of God" (2 Corinthians 5:21).

What Happens When We Sin?

Dear Believer,

What happens when we sin? Are we immediately out of favor with God? Are we out of fellowship? When we do something wrong, whether in disobedience, negligence or ignorance, are we now back within in the grasp of the enemy?

Read what 1 John 2:1 states,

> **"My dear children, I write this to you so that you will not sin. But if anybody does sin, we have an advocate with the Father—Jesus Christ, the Righteousness One. He is the atoning sacrifice for our sins, and not only ours but also for the sins of the whole world."**
>
> (New International Version)

How many times have we given in to the concept that because I've sinned I'm just a failure. The guilt alone is enough to drive us into hiding, just like Adam and Eve. We must realize that sinning is not an excuse to run away from

God, but to run to Him. Why? Because He stands ready to wash us from our sins every time.

"If we confess our sins, he is faithful and just to forgive us our sins, and to cleanse us from all unrighteousness."

(1 John 1:9 King James Version)

<u>Satan is no longer in control of our sins.</u> We are now God's children in every respect. He takes care of all our needs, even the need to be washed from sin. Jesus said, "Unless I wash you, you have no part with me" (John 13:8 New International Version). It is expected that we will often need washing, both in our natural bodies and in our spirits. No one in their right mind neglects their daily responsibility of personal hygiene. Likewise, Jesus isn't bothered with the numerous washings needed for our spirits. He cleanses us from **all** unrighteousness and we are once again righteous.

The Integrity of Words

Dear Believer,

In Isaiah 55:11, God makes a statement that tells us how certain He is of the integrity of His Word. He states,

> "It shall not return unto me void, but it shall accomplish that which I please, and it shall prosper in the thing whereto I sent it."
>
> (King James Version)

Years later, Jesus spoke to a fig tree and the next day the disciples were amazed that it had fallen on its side. The power of His speech was obviously far beyond anything they had ever experienced. To this very day, we stand in awe of the power of the words of God. What is even more startling is the notion that God has given us access to the same words and the same results. Listen closely to the words of Jesus,

> "Whosoever shall say unto this mountain, Be thou removed and be thou cast into the sea; and shall

not doubt in his heart, <u>but shall believe that those things which he saith shall come to pass</u>; he shall have whatsoever he saith."

(Mark 11:23)

Jesus starts this statement with the words, "Have faith in God," or use the God kind of faith. What is the God kind of faith? God believes His words will never come back empty or void. It's time for believers to step up and follow our Father's example. Will you dare to say, "I'm like my Father. My words don't return to me void." This is a new level. Come on up!

Have the God Kind of Faith

Dear Believer,

In the very first verses of the Bible, the account of creation is written. Often read in children's Sunday School, these verses have been considered more fantasy than anything else. Even believers find it a bit of a stretch to believe that this kind of thing could actually happen. Some have chalked it up to be another religious tale that has little bearing on reality. Read what the Bible says in Genesis 1:1-3,

> "In the beginning God created the heaven and the earth. And the earth was without form, and void; and darkness was upon the face of the deep. And the Spirit of God moved upon the face of the waters. And God said, Let there be light: and there was light."

Is this the beginning of just another fairy tale or is there any serious revelation here? I believe you'll find the words of Jesus revealing when you read Mark 11:22,23.

> "And Jesus answering saith unto them, Have faith in God. For verily I say unto you, That whosoever

shall say unto this mountain, Be thou removed, and be thou cast into the sea; and shall not doubt in his heart, but shall believe that those things which he saith shall come to pass; he shall have whatsoever he saith."

Greek scholars have told us what Jesus was saying was, "Have the God kind of faith." Why would Jesus tell ordinary people to exercise the God kind of faith? It's because God is our Father and we are growing up to be like Him. We might as well begin to talk like our "Daddy." Don't hesitate to speak to the mountain (no matter what the mountain may be) and believe that your words are coming to pass. Jesus said <u>**whoever**</u> does this will have <u>**whatever**</u> they say. If that sounds like fantasy, Jesus makes things worse by adding **"and nothing shall be impossible unto you"** (Matthew 17:20).

It is interesting to note that babies learning to walk like their parents fall many times on their first attempts, but that <u>never</u> stops them. They instinctively know that they have the capacity to stand upright and eventually they walk. Maybe you've had that kind of experience when you attempted to speak in faith. Don't be discouraged. Falling down is just a prelude to walking.

The Process

Dear Believer,

Jesus often used natural things and processes to give insight into the realm of the spirit. He informed His disciples that there was a discernable process by which everything, including miracles, comes to pass. This process is like a man planting seed. After time has elapsed, the Word comes to pass in stages. This process is not instantaneous as some suppose, but takes time to materialize. And although it takes time, it's still supernatural. Our challenge is <u>not to miss the supernatural looking for the spectacular</u>.

Everyone would like to perform the instant miracles Jesus did. But even Jesus was subject to the time requirements connected to the miraculous. When he healed the sick, it was the <u>completion</u> of the process begun years earlier. It was just like a man planting seed. As a matter of fact Jesus said the whole "kingdom" operates according to this system. Learn this system and you become eligible to receive the same results. This is what Jesus said;

> "So is the kingdom of God, as if a man should cast seed into the ground; And should sleep, and rise night and day, and the seed should spring and grow up, he knoweth not how. For the earth bringeth forth fruit of herself; first the blade, then the ear, after that the full corn in the ear. But when the fruit is brought forth, immediately he putteth in the sickle, because the harvest is come."
>
> (Mark 4:26-29)

It was a revelation that when Jesus healed the sick he was bringing to pass the words of Isaiah, who said, **"He took our infirmities, and bare our sicknesses"** (Isaiah 53:4, Matthew 8:17). It's surprising to note that the actions of Jesus were a direct result of words which had been spoken many years earlier. Just like seeds, those words grew to become reality. Your words are designed to produce the same outcome. Believe the words you say are like seeds being planted and **"nothing will be impossible unto you"** (Matthew 17:20).

The Road to the Miraculous

Dear Believer,

Don't be disturbed by the struggle that ensues whenever you take a stand on God's Word. Whether it is for your healing or finances or any promise God has made, you can count on some form of opposition. While everyone who has lived any time for the Lord knows this, we sometimes forget that taking a stand also places us <u>on the road to the miraculous</u>. The enemy knows that if he is to have any chance of stopping us, he must interrupt the process by which God's promises come to pass.

Jesus knew we needed some insight into this process. He explained it in a simple story (or parable) of a man planting seed. Whenever we hear and take a stand on God's promises, the seed is planted and there is a set time for harvest. God's miraculous seed will come to pass for you if you understand this simple process. Jesus said,

"Now the parable is this: The seed is the word of God. Those by the way side are they that hear; then cometh the devil, and taketh away the word out of their hearts, lest they should believe and be saved. They on the rock are they, which, when they hear, receive the word with joy; and these have no root, which for a while believe, and in time of temptation fall away. And that which fell among thorns are they, which, when they have heard, go forth, and are choked with cares and riches and pleasures of this life, and bring no fruit to perfection. But that on the good ground are they, which in an honest and good heart, having heard the word, keep it, and bring forth fruit with patience."

(Luke 8:11-15)

The Word of God is incorruptible seed (1 Peter 1:23). It will accomplish whatever it says. But it must remain in good ground in order to perform its miraculous work. As the receivers of God's Word, we are responsible here. Satan knows this and is trying everything within his ability to remove the seed. We, not Satan, control the outcome every time.

Be diligent to keep the word you have heard by meditating, memorizing and studying. Give the Word the best part of your day, not the time when you're too tired. If protected,

God's Word will produce miraculous results in your life. Remember this Old Testament verse:

"He that goeth forth and weepeth, bearing precious seed, shall doubtless come again with rejoicing, bringing his sheaves with him."

(Psalm 126:6)

The Enemy in My Thoughts

Dear Believer,

God always speaks of things that seem impossible to us. When we decide to believe Him, we quickly learn that our natural thinking is neither friendly to nor cooperative with His words. Natural thinking seems harmless but opposes the things of the spirit. The natural mind is the <u>enemy</u> of God.

Romans 8:7 states, "**The carnal mind is enmity against God: for it is not subject to the law of God, neither indeed can be.**"

From the time of your childhood, the enemy has had years to infiltrate your thinking. His plan was to keep you within the boundaries of the natural world, where you can be dominated. Now we must cleanse our thoughts if we expect to achieve the impossible. Just as everyday there is a need for physical washing, everyday there is also a need to wash your mind from carnal or natural thinking. Some of us would never dream of allowing any odor to remain in our bodies. Why then would we allow "stinkin' thinkin'" to remain in our thoughts.

> "Thou wilt keep him in perfect peace, whose mind is stayed on thee: because he trusteth in thee."
>
> (Isaiah 26:3)
>
> "For the weapons of our warfare are not carnal, but mighty through God to the pulling down of strong holds; Casting down imaginations, and every high thing that exalteth itself against the knowledge of God, and bringing into captivity every thought to the obedience of Christ."
>
> (2 Corinthians 10:4)

You cannot expect to have a good day today unless you stop and take control of your thought life. If you don't, your circumstances will take the lead and you will bow to the tyranny of pressing issues, difficult problems, unforeseen emergencies.

As the scripture above states, God has given us powerful weapons that destroy every thought that opposes His Word. You have the power to select godly thoughts and to reject others. Use your weapons to destroy the stronghold that the enemy set up in your mind years ago.

Winning Is Our Family Tradition

Dear Believer,

In any sport you can find two types of players, those who came to play and those who came to win. The person who said, "It's not whether you win or lose, but how you play the game" was probably trying to console someone who lost. In great athletes, there is a noticeable capacity to focus on the goal and to keep at it until it is attained. Your Father, God Almighty, has a reputation for winning. His victory over Satan at Calvary is the greatest of all time. Accordingly, he has not planned not even one defeat for our lives. We are the offspring of an individual who never loses a battle. Winning is our family tradition.

God told Israel, **"No weapon that is formed against thee shall prosper"** (Isaiah 54:17). Jesus said, **"If you have faith...nothing shall be impossible to you"** (Matthew 17:20). These are not the statements of those who would settle for a consolation prize. Reaching the goal and winning is important to God and should be important to you.

Paul said,

"Brethren, I count not myself to have apprehended: but this one thing I do, forgetting those things which are behind, and reaching forth unto those things which are before, I press toward the mark for the prize of the high calling of God in Christ Jesus."

(Philippians 3:13,14)

Paul was a winner. Key to his success was the fact that he knew how to forget the past and press toward the prize.

As you strive toward your goal, beware of the distractions that can knock you off course. As Joshua came near to the land they had waited so long to possess, the Lord commanded them not to lose focus. He said,

"This book of the law shall not depart out of thy mouth; but thou shalt <u>meditate therein day and night</u>, that thou mayest observe to do according to all that is written therein: for then thou shalt make thy way prosperous, and <u>then thou shalt have good success</u>."

(Joshua 1:8)

If God is for you who can be against you?

Take Time and Meditate

Dear Believer,

Joshua is such a great example for anyone who has held on to faith. He served Moses for many years and witnessed great miracles God performed for the children of Israel such as the parting of the Red Sea and the manna from Heaven. He also experienced the disappointment of being so close to the Promised Land, but unable to enter. Surprisingly, it was not a lack of faith on his part, but doubt and fear from those around him. Both he and Caleb believed God, but had to turn away from their dream and return to the wilderness for another 40 years. It would take that long for the doubters to die. These days few of us can imagine waiting for anything for 40 years, but Joshua persevered.

He withstood this long ordeal with faith intact and returned to the Jordan for the second time. In Joshua 1:1-9, after the death of the beloved Moses, God speaks directly to him. (This is a great passage to read and reread. God was no longer speaking to a young man, but to an elderly man (80 plus) who had continued to believe His Word. Apparently, real faith can stand the test of time. This time as God spoke, He repeated His promises and He added, **"be strong and of good courage."** Fear is what made the people miss the mark the first time. God was saying to Joshua, "It's time; we're there! Time to take the land. This time don't allow any fear."

It was great advice because the task ahead was yet a challenge to their faith and their courage. In this passage, God also took the opportunity to reveal to Joshua a secret to prosperity. Meditate on the Word day and night. If we not only read, but also meditate on the Word of God, we will make our way prosperous and successful. I'm glad for this insight, aren't you. Let's not be hearers only of this blessing. Take quality time and meditate on the promises of God.

Prepare For the Glory

Dear Believer,

One of the most inspiring moments of my life was having the opportunity to preach in a men's prison. The place was packed with men from all races and all walks of life. They worshipped God unashamedly with praises that could be heard before you entered the prison gates. I was so moved by these men who had fallen into terrible predicaments, but had given their lives totally to Jesus. They spoke with purpose in their voices and the love of God in their eyes. I cannot forget the experience.

We must all begin to more fully grasp the fact that we have God's actual likeness and God's image. We are the only beings that have been given such an honor and privilege by God himself. We are not filled with the spirit of angels but with His divine nature (2 Peter 1:4). His design for our lives is that we should be like Him. We should never be shy or bashful about speaking God's words, adopting His ways or acting like our Father. Why would He give us His words,

His spirit and His name if He didn't plan for us to be like Him in every way. Look at the following scripture;

> **"Behold, what manner of love the Father hath bestowed upon us, that we should be called the sons of God: therefore the world knoweth us not, because it knew him not. Beloved, now are we the sons of God, and it doth not yet appear what we shall be: but we know that, when he shall appear, <u>we shall be like him</u>; for we shall see him as he is."**
>
> (1 John 3:1-2)

God has given us a position so high; it's difficult to conceive. That we should actually be in the God class and members of God's own family. But we are. And it's by God's own doing that we are. Resist the mindset of the <u>pitiful</u> and take your place in the family of the <u>powerful</u>. God wants you to reign in this life (Romans 5:17). So, prepare yourself for the glory.

Wisdom for Long Trials

"Today if ye will hear his voice, harden not your hearts."

(Hebrews 4:7)

Dear Believer,

One painful lesson derived from the wilderness experience of the Israelites is, "Don't allow the hard things you've experienced to harden your spirit against God." Some who endure hard tests and trials display a telltale hardness of spirit, a bitterness and cynicism from years of battle and hardship. When they talk of their experiences with God and His promises, a stale air of doubt is present. It's as if their experiences have taught them to live according to the Word of God, but to expect very little. They are quick to warn you, "Don't get your hopes up. You don't want to get disappointed." While others who endure hard trials and tests seem to increase in a sweet childlike trust in the Lord, maintaining an air of expectancy and excitement everyday. What's the difference between the two? The latter have not allowed their trials to harden their hearts.

For some of us, our trials have been long in duration, and time between conflicts has been short. If we're not watchful, this can provide the pretext for discouragement to enter. And, because our "due season" has been long in coming, we can allow our confidence in the Word of God to wane. This is the time to be very watchful. Don't lose focus on the goal. Make up in your mind that quitting is not an option, that you will stand until the victory comes. The scripture in Galatians 6:9 states "we shall reap if we faint not." When we make the quality decision not to quit, the next event is "due season."

Naturally thinking, we have the right to be battle weary. But those who know God know that it's not our strength we are relying on. If you're experiencing weariness from a long ordeal, do what David did. He said, "The Lord is the strength of my life" (Psalm 27:1). David learned the secret of tapping into God's strength to complete those long journeys. Take time and read Psalm 27 and tap into that strength for yourself.

Walk By Faith Not By Sight

Dear Believer,

I thank God often for my sight. To be able to see bright sunshine, green trees, white clouds and blue sky is a wonderful gift that I don't take for granted. One only has to see someone who does not have the gift of sight to appreciate this blessing even more. Without it, we would have to feel our way along. But as wonderful as sight is, it can be a major hindrance when we begin to develop faith in God. The Bible states, **"Faith is the substance of things hoped for and the evidence of things <u>not seen</u>"** (Hebrews 11:1) and, in 2 Corinthians 5:7, **"We walk by faith, not by sight."**

Faith is the ability to trust in things we cannot see. It is essential to walking with God. As a matter of fact, without faith we cannot please God. (Please read Hebrews 11:6). In this world, we need our eyesight but we need faith even more. Faith takes us beyond the natural limits of sight into the realm where God exists and operates. Developing faith is like flying so high above the earth you no longer rely on eyesight, but on the accuracy of your instruments. It's the higher way of living that God designed for every believer. It's living by trusting what God says instead of what you see. God always sees much farther up the road than we can. Let's trust His sight and develop our faith.

How do I develop my faith? **"Faith cometh by hearing, and hearing by the word of God"** (Romans 10:17). Take time routinely to hear and read God's words. This will give you insight into God's promises for you in this life. Then speak His words and meditate on what He says. Take the time to develop your faith. You won't regret the time you spend at this. Eventually what you see will take a backseat to what you believe. As precious as sight is, don't let your eyes dictate your life. Instead, let what you believe be your guide. Repeat this sentence, "No matter what the circumstances, what I feel or see, the Word is working mightily in me."

Believing To See

Dear Believer,

Here's a familiar passage of scripture I'd like you to read:

> "'You will not certainly die,' the serpent said to the woman. 'For God knows that when you eat of it your <u>eyes will be opened</u>, and you will be like God, knowing good and evil.' When the woman saw that the fruit of the tree was good for food and <u>pleasing to the eye</u>, and also desirable for gaining wisdom, she took some and ate it. She also gave some to her husband, who was with her, and he ate it. Then the <u>eyes</u> of both of them were opened, and they realized they were naked."
>
> (Genesis 3:4-7 New International Version)

This is the account of the tragic event that forever changed the way we see things in this life. In this passage, Adam and Eve are conned by Satan into believing if they disobeyed God's words, their eyes would be "opened." That they would begin to see things like God Himself. Little did they know they were already seeing through God's eyes. We believe they were surrounded by the glory of God, which covered their nakedness. Satan's plot was to rob them of the divine sight they possessed, forever damaging their ability to see the things of God clearly. To their utter regret, after being duped by the words of the Devil, they never regained their divine eyesight.

Instead they entered a world where what they could see brought both fear and condemnation.

This is the same thing the enemy is doing against the children of God today. He is trying to keep us looking at the wrong things. If we are not watchful, what we see happening around us will dictate what we believe. That's not God's way of doing things (2 Corinthians 5:7). It's the way of natural fallen man. But when we walk with God, we must put the things we see in proper perspective. Frustration and fear always follows when we focus on our circumstances. Even believers who have walked with God for some time can fall into this trap. We must begin to exercise the power of "believing to see." David said, **"I had fainted, unless I had believed to see the goodness of the LORD in the land of the living"** (Psalm 27:13 King James Version).

Your faith in what God says will defeat every force in this world. Don't faint! Believe to see the goodness of the Lord! I know it's not easy. But if you will do it, victory will come to you.

John 5:4 states, **"and this is the victory that overcometh the world, even our faith."**

Competing for High Stakes

Dear Believer,

Very few people enjoy watching two mismatched teams play a game that ends in a lopsided score. Those games are not worth watching and sometimes, even before the game is concluded, the fans at the stadium begin leaving the stands for home. But when a championship is on the line, whatever the sport, people will pay dearly for the chance to watch the spectacle unfold. When the best players in their field go all out against a worthy opponent, this is competition at its best. When teams play to determine the true champions, it is history in the making. The excitement generated by game time builds up to heart pounding anticipation infecting both the players and the crowd alike. And, when the stakes are high no one wants to lose.

In Christ, we are combating an enemy who is fiercely competitive. The stakes are so high he is contesting our every move toward victory. This is the conflict which determines who will rule in our lives, now and in the future. Our enemy would love to add us to his list of victims he has successfully "devoured." And we cannot afford to lose if we expect to forever rid our lives of his destructive influence. He is battling to keep us under his cloud of defeat and deception. As you fight, keep in mind the fact that in close contests, the lead can change hands several times. And sometimes the momentum changes when the opposing team scores with a maneuver we didn't expect. Don't allow yourself to waver because of unexpected advances by the enemy. Experienced players know that this is just the ebb and flow of great competition. Victory is ours!

Set your sights on winning. It is the only acceptable option for the believer. Remember, **"No weapon formed against you shall prosper"** (Isaiah 54:17). **"Greater is he that is in you, than he that is in the world"** (1 John 4:4). **"Whatsoever is born of God overcomes the world; and this is he victory that overcomes the world, even our faith"** (1 John 5:4). **"Resist the devil, and he will flee from you"** (James 4:7).

Lord, What's Taking So Long?

Dear Believer,

If you're like me you question sometimes the reason things take so much time to manifest in God. Why is it that when we stand on a promise or pray for something to happen there is often a delay before it comes to pass?

Some people don't even ask because they believe He either won't answer or they'll have to wait a long time for an answer. Is God always slow in answering? Look at this verse of scripture:

> "The Lord is not slow in keeping his promise, as some understand slowness. Instead he is patient with you, not wanting anyone to perish."
>
> (2 Peter 3:9 New International Version)

God is not the one who is slow. He desires us to receive every promise. It was His idea to make great promises to us so that His children could receive the best He has. (Please take time now to read 2 Corinthians 1:20 & 2 Peter 1:4).

We're the ones holding up the action! Every good parent desires to give good things to their children right now. But we also know that children must learn while growing. No one wants to spend any time with a selfish, spoiled child. Neither do any of us want our children to be stunted in their growth.

And unfortunately, these days there are also those who prey upon innocent children who are unaware of the danger they pose. As a result, God's promises must also, of necessity, double as "teachable moments," times when the Lord teaches us survival skills.

The first lesson we learn is obedience. Obeying God is both critical and profitable. Since we know God loves us, obeying Him, even in difficult situations always leads to blessings. Disobedience to God results in disappointment and misery. Not because of God's eagerness to punish us, but because we have an enemy who is waiting to take advantage of any open door. Our fore-parents, Adam and Eve, forfeited an entire world of blessings by disobeying. They were blind to the fact that by that same act of disobedience they had opened the door to Satan who immediately took them both captive.

God wants you to receive His promises. His desire is to see you walk in them right away. But, He also knows there is an enemy lurking about to take advantage of any slip-ups.

So don't complain about the time it takes to receive God's promises. Thank God for it. Use the time to learn the lesson God's teaching you right now. Ask Him, "Lord show me what I'm to learn while I'm waiting."

What's The Hold Up?

Dear Believer,

We do our best to fight the feeling, but sometimes we do feel impatient waiting for the manifestation of God's promises. Recently in prayer, I asked the Lord about the experience I had been having with the words I speak. Why is it that our words are often hindered while His words always hit their mark right away? What the Lord shared with me was a little surprising. He said to me, "I'm getting the same results you're getting. We are in this together. Both of us are experiencing these delays."

For years, I have held the view that God always gets whatever He says no matter what. God had to remind me that His powerful Word is released or held up depending largely upon our faith. "With his stripes we are healed" (Isaiah 53:5) is a powerful promise that will heal the sick. But, as powerful as it is, it's power will be postponed until someone believes and acts on it. His words are full of power. He is not holding back on us. But, He has chosen the power of

<u>our</u> faith as the determining factor in this process. Read Matthew 17:20 King James Version:

> **"And Jesus said unto them, If ye have faith as a grain of mustard seed, ye shall say unto this mountain, Remove hence to yonder place; and it shall remove; and nothing shall be impossible unto you."**

Everything we receive, from salvation to daily provisions, is held up until we release our faith. For whatever length of time faith is missing, the promise is delayed. This affects both our ability to receive and God's scriptural authority to release it to us.

After four hundred years of slavery in Egypt and forty years in the wilderness, how could God's chosen people fail to enter the land God promised? It's almost inconceivable that an entire generation died never receiving the promise. Instead, God had to wait an additional forty years for their children to grow up before His words were finally believed, removing the hold up.

Kenneth Hagin once said, "Speaking words of faith and thinking thoughts of faith will deliver the soul out of defeat into victory."

Waiting in His Presence

Dear Believer,

Here's one of my favorite passages of scripture;

> "Hast thou not known? hast thou not heard, that the everlasting God, the LORD, the Creator of the ends of the earth, fainteth not, neither is weary? there is no searching of his understanding. He giveth power to the faint; and to them that have no might he increaseth strength. Even the youths shall faint and be weary, and the young men shall utterly fall: But they that wait upon the LORD shall renew their strength; they shall mount up with wings as eagles; they shall run, and not be weary; and they shall walk, and not faint."
>
> (Isaiah 40:28-31)

Waiting on the Lord is wonderful when you know that you will be given power while you're waiting. Each great move of God in the earth was preceded by a time of waiting. Moses spent forty days waiting and God gave him the commandments on tables of stone that we still live by today. Jesus waited in the wilderness and afterward "returned in the power of the spirit" to perform great miracles (Luke 4:14). His disciples waited in the upper room after His resurrection for weeks and were suddenly filled with power from on high (Acts 2:4).

While we are waiting in God's presence communicating with Him and appreciating His goodness, something is happening. It may not be seen or felt at the time, but an impartation from the Lord takes place as we wait in His presence. That means that God is supernaturally imparting something you need as you wait. God gives <u>power to the faint</u> and when you feel you can't go on, He <u>increases your strength</u>. How can we wait on God? By taking time to communicate with God in prayer and meditation, and to give Him thanks and praise. This acknowledges Him, causing Him to bring His ability into our predicaments. What more could we ask? With His ability nothing is impossible.

Be encouraged. Because you have waited on the Lord for a season, expect a supernatural surge in your strength. Expect to run and not be weary and to walk and not faint. That's the way God operates.

A Certain Amount

Dear Believer,

"A certain amount, it takes a certain amount!" These are the first words the Lord spoke to me as I woke up one morning. He informed me that every project or challenge takes a certain amount of praying, saying and doing to get the desired result. But the desired result will always follow the right amount. Even in tough times when the situation seems too hard to tackle. A certain amount of prayer and fasting will do the job. This is what Jesus shared with His disciples, who were bewildered when they failed to cast out a stubborn demon. **"This kind goeth not out but by prayer and fasting"** (Matthew 17: 21).

Where did we get the notion that with just one command from us the Devil would be sent packing? Having learned of the awesome power of speaking the name of Jesus, it as though we expect to wave a magic wand and everything immediately changes. What we have is not magic, but it is awesome power. Jesus himself had to resist temptation not once, but three times to defeat the Devil. But the third time was enough to make him leave for an entire season. **"And when the devil had ended all the temptation, he departed from him for a season"** (Luke 4:13). In Isaiah 55:10, God revealed to us that His Word is like rain that falls from the clouds. Rain is vitally important to all of us, yet it doesn't happen just because there is moisture in the air. There must be a significant amount of water vapor rising and it must be cooled at the right temperature before the rain begins to fall. If God's Word is like that, it's a mistake to think that a hit or miss approach to reading or speaking God's Word will do anything more than ward off the enemy temporarily. If we expect a breakthrough in our lives, we must be willing to do what it takes to get it. Be wise; better results often require increased effort. For tenacious adversity or infirmity, try taking the Word like medicine every few hours accompanied with daily communion. God never loses.

Spending the Time Required

Dear Believer,

Sometimes we expect God to deliver regardless of the fact that we haven't spent the time required to receive the answer. Some conversations take longer than others. It is very rude to leave while someone is talking to you, especially when it's God. Simple explanations are usually much shorter than complicated ones. We must take the time required to get a clear message from the Lord. God told me each challenge and each project takes "a certain amount" to achieve the goal. When we pursue significant promises from God, we have an enemy who loves to discourage us by resisting our every effort. And since he is undetectable to our natural vision, we can get discouraged after a long delay. Please read this condensed excerpt of the tenth chapter of Daniel to see this point.

> "In the third year of Cyrus king of Persia, a revelation was given to Daniel (who was called Belteshazzar). Its message was true and it concerned a great war. The understanding of the message came to him

> in a vision. At that time I, Daniel, mourned for three weeks. I ate no choice food; no meat or wine touched my lips; and I used no lotions at all until the three weeks were over.... Then he continued, "Do not be afraid, Daniel. Since the first day that you set your mind to gain understanding and to humble yourself before your God, your words were heard, and I have come in response to them. But the prince of the Persian kingdom resisted me twenty-one days.
>
> Then Michael, one of the chief princes, came to help me, because I was detained."
>
> (Daniel 10:1-3;12-13 New International Version)

Daniel was a devout man of God who prayed three times daily. But even such a committed man of God experienced the delay caused by demonic resistance. Fortunately, he knew enough about God to stay the course in his consecration. God never loses. Demonic resistance is futile. This challenge required twenty-one days before the breakthrough, but Daniel was up to the task. Just like Daniel, if we persist for the time required for our breakthrough, it will come. We don't always know what is interfering with the blessing God promised us. But we can rest assured it's not God falling short on His promise. Set your heart never to give up! God's Word never fails. Never!

Using the Little You've Got

> "God hath chosen the foolish things of the world to confound the wise; and God hath chosen the weak things of the world to confound the things which are mighty; And base things of the world, and things which are despised, hath God chosen, yea, and things which are not, to bring to nought things that are: That no flesh should glory in his presence."
>
> (1 Corinthians 1:27-29 King James Version)

Dear Believer,

These verses articulate God's penchant for using insignificant things to defeat overwhelming adversaries. The enemy loves to flaunt his size, intelligence or numerical superiority. But it never matters to God how big, smart or numerous the enemy appears to be. God chooses to humble His arrogant foe by adding His awesome power to the actions of mortal men. Because we are often so outmatched, we seem like "sheep for the slaughter," but we are more than conquerors through the God that loves us (Romans 8:36-37).

In the time of David, a small stone was used to defeat a nine-foot man of war. No one expected David to come out the victor, but with God's unseen support, he prevailed. He knew that when you have a covenant with God whatever you have available at the time can be used to defeat your enemy. He killed a giant with a small stone. Using what is available right now is the whole point of the matter. We should not fall for the deception that everything must be provided before we can move. God often expects His people to step forward without seeing provision. That's just the way God works. We must have the faith to step out, believing in the provision of our unseen Creator. Please take time and read Psalm 91.

This is difficult for people who have a perceived need to see the full provision before venturing forth. But such individuals always have a difficult time walking with God. Without faith it is impossible to please him (Hebrews 11:6). Faith in the unseen is a skill we must all master. You may not have much, but you can take a step and use what you've got.

Use Whatever God Provided

> "Jonathan said to his young armor-bearer, "Come, let's go over to the outpost of those uncircumcised fellows. Perhaps the LORD will act in our behalf. Nothing can hinder the LORD from saving, whether by many or by few."
>
> (1 Samuel 14:6 New International Version)

Dear Believer,

In this scriptural passage, facing insurmountable odds and perilous circumstances, Jonathan, Kings Saul's son, takes a totally unexpected action that leads to a miraculous turnaround. Saul had been king for only a short time when the Philistine army came against him. Thousands of trained well-equipped soldiers poured into Israel to make quick work of this inexperienced, newly appointed novice and his rag tag army. Angered by the attempt to throw off the yoke of their rule, the Philistines had a score to settle. The outcome was certain to be a disaster for Saul and anyone who followed him. Worse still, the scriptures record that when it came time for battle there was neither sword nor spear to be found in all of Israel, except with Saul and Jonathan. This was not going to be a battle but a slaughter. After taking one look at what appeared to be certain death, the men of Israel hid themselves in any covering they could find. All that remained with Saul were a few hundred very fearful men. Only one individual refused to fear, Jonathan. (Please read 1 Samuel 13 and 14).

He refused to be affected by the hopeless circumstances terrorizing everyone else. He knew the covenant he had with God; the enemy will come out against you one way and flee before you seven ways (Deuteronomy 28:7). He also knew that God never requires much to defeat the enemy. Jonathan therefore took the one sword he had along with his armor-bearer and stepped toward his enemy. Using what little he had was enough to get God Almighty on the scene. Moved by Jonathan's action, God sent an earthquake shaking the very ground they stood on, sending them into panic. Thousands of Philistines were defeated that day by essentially an army without weapons.

God is eager to do the same thing for each of us. But we must be willing to use the little we have. We can't always wait for full provisions. Start toward the enemy with what God has already provided. It's time for God to show you that, **"My grace is sufficient for you, for my power is made perfect in weakness"** (2 Corinthians 12:9).

God's Way

"For my thoughts are not your thoughts, neither are your ways my ways, saith the LORD. For as the heavens are higher than the earth, so are my ways higher than your ways, and my thoughts than your thoughts."

(Isaiah 55:8-9 King James Version)

Dear Believer,

Many of us have heard this scripture from time to time. It holds no great surprises for us that God's ways and thoughts are higher than ours.

Because He's God, we have resigned ourselves to that fact. But did you know that in this same chapter He reveals to us His way of doing things? He says,

"For as the rain cometh down, and the snow from heaven, and returneth not thither, but watereth the earth, and maketh it bring forth and bud, that it may give seed to the sower, and bread to the eater: So shall my word be that goeth forth out of my mouth:

> it shall not return unto me void, but it shall accomplish that which I please, and it shall prosper in the thing whereto I sent it."
>
> (Isaiah 55:10-11)

God compares His Word to the effectiveness of rain. It falls from the heavenly clouds above, transforming the earth below, <u>making it</u> bring forth and bud. Although rainy days can cause us some inconvenience, we all know how much we rely on rain for our food. How does God do things? He sends His Word. He states, **"It (My Word) shall accomplish that which I please."** God is absolutely certain that His Word <u>will accomplish</u>.

God demonstrated from the very beginning of time that it takes His words to create things. It's recorded that our entire world was made by them (Genesis 1). Having proven the creative potential of His Word, God then displayed an almost unimaginable grace to actually bestow the same ability upon us.

In the scriptures, He has shown His children the exact way to create as He has, but to access it we must go back and revisit some things. Let's take some time to think about the range of possibilities that accompany access to God's creative words. Take time and think about what you desire to create in this world and bring it before God in prayer.

Seeds

Dear Believer,

In Isaiah 55:8 God said, "My ways are not your ways." Then He describes His way of doing things. God does everything thing by sending His Word (John 1:3). He describes His words as if each one is alive and on the move. He says, **"it shall accomplish that which I please, and it shall prosper in the thing whereto I sent it"** (verse 11). God is so certain of its effectiveness, He guarantees that it never returns empty handed or **"void."** The exciting thing about it is He's actually given us direct use of that same awesome creative power. It is truly amazing that ordinary people can use His words like a simple farmer uses seed and reap a supernatural harvest. Look at the following scripture:

> "The farmer sows the word. Some people are like seed along the path, where the word is sown. As soon as they hear it, Satan comes and takes away the word that was sown in them. Others, like seed sown on rocky places, hear the word and at once receive it with joy. But since they have no root, they

last only a short time. When trouble or persecution comes because of the word, they quickly fall away. Still others, like seed sown among thorns, hear the word; but the worries of this life, the deceitfulness of wealth and the desires for other things come in and choke the word, making it unfruitful. Others, like seed sown on good soil, hear the word, accept it, and produce a crop—thirty, sixty or even a hundred times what was sown."

(Mark 4:14-20 New International Version)

In this simple parable, God is revealing the process words undergo as they make their way into physical manifestation. It's like seeds growing into harvest. Take time and really get this insight. It will really bless you.

Keep Watch Over Your Words

Dear Believer,

"Seeds" (God's promises) for whatever you desire must be sown first into your heart by saying them aloud. Those spoken words must remain in place for a required season. Whoever will keep watch over their words not allowing doubt or distraction, but acting like God's Word is true, will experience supernatural manifestation. This is God's way of bringing things to pass. This has been His pattern throughout history. This must now be our pattern as well.

Everyone loves to receive miracles. But few want to invest the time and effort required to create them. But it's time to train ourselves more diligently in this process so that we can cooperate with God's Word to produce more of them. This will require patience and wisdom but the miraculous rewards are worth every minute of our efforts.

We have all been made aware that using God's Word is not without fierce opposition. While His Word will ultimately defeat any enemy attack, it will not prevent a desperate backlash. Be prepared when the circumstances appear to get worse after the Word is applied to your situation. Your enemy knows that because of the certainty of God's Word, his only hope is to somehow snatch that creative power out of your mouth and heart. But if you resist his attempt at interference by standing your ground with God's Word in your heart and continually coming from your lips, your supernatural harvest is guaranteed (James 4:7).

The Manifestation Process

Dear Believer,

It's so good when Jesus shares with us kingdom principles that govern both the spiritual and natural world. These principles are keys to operating the way our Father does and getting the same results he gets. Here is one such principle.

> "And he said, So is the kingdom of God, as if a man should cast seed into the ground; And should sleep, and rise night and day, and the seed should spring and grow up, he knoweth not how. For the earth bringeth forth fruit of herself; first the blade, then the ear, after that the full corn in the ear. But when the fruit is brought forth, immediately he putteth in the sickle, because the harvest is come."
>
> (Mark 4:26-29)

Jesus reveals here that you should know that there is a three-part process involved in the manifestation of your miracle. First the blade, then the ear, then the full corn. Did you know that your answer can come in stages? How often have we shrunk back from our faith when we ask for something grand and see only a small piece of it emerge? That's not a reason to doubt, but to rejoice. Out of the ground first appears a small blade. It may be a phone call from a person you haven't spoken to in ages. Or, for no reason, someone may give you a small contribution as seed toward what you are believing God for. It has little resemblance to the end product. It's not an abundance, but it is the beginning of the harvest.

Don't give up or be discouraged when experiencing these stages of the manifestation. For some reason we have been taught to believe that miracles are always immediate. But we can miss the supernatural looking for the spectacular. Jesus is showing us here that the whole kingdom is like a man planting seed, not knowing exactly how the seed is going to be transformed into the final product. But the guarantee is that, even though he doesn't know how it's done, the cycle always ends in harvest. That is, if we don't faint (Galatians 6:9).

> **"He that goeth forth and weepeth, bearing precious seed, shall doubtless come again with rejoicing bringing his sheaves with him."**
>
> (Psalm 126:6)

Almost Too Good To Be True

Dear Believer,

Sometimes what we learn in the Gospel is so good it seems too good to be true. Did you know that God has always intended for you to be like Him?

Yes, just like Him! John wrote, "we know when he shall appear we shall be like him" (1 John 3:2). It sounds almost unbelievable that God Almighty should even consider transforming us into His likeness. But when you think about it, from the very beginning He showed what He really designed for us. Genesis 1:26 states, "And God said, Let us make man after our image, after our likeness and let them have dominion."

God, who is very protective of His image and likeness, never allows anyone to make any wooden or stone statues of Himself (Exodus 20:4). But He intentionally designed man (Genesis 1:27) to be just like Him, to have His very image. He would then continue to rule Heaven and mankind would begin to rule the earth. Adam had so much authority; even his mistakes affected the entire world. And as we all know he made a big mistake disobeying God. As a result, the whole human race fell under the authority of the outlaw, Satan.

Centuries have come and gone since that fateful misstep, but God has never forgotten His original design. He is yet determined that we are to be like Him. And, He has yet provided a way for us to actually experience His likeness. We can walk in His divine nature simply by believing and acting upon His promises. Look at the following passage:

> **"According as his divine power hath given UNTO US all things that pertain unto life and godliness, through the knowledge of him that hath CALLED US to glory and virtue: Whereby are given UNTO US exceeding great and precious promises: that by these ye might be partakers of the divine nature, having escaped the corruption that is in the world through lust."**
>
> (2 Peter 1:3-4)

If you haven't done so already, get in the Word and get some of those promises and begin to speak them, memorize them and meditate on them. If you are already doing this, increase your efforts. Let's take Him up on His offer.

Faith Beyond Hopelessness

Dear Believer,

For so long the Lord searched for someone who would have the kind of faith He needed to bring salvation into the earth. He found that individual in Abraham. The kind of faith Abraham displayed was the kind that would believe what God said no matter what the circumstances; faith that would believe God even in the face of hopelessness. Anyone can believe God when the things He's saying can be seen coming in the distance. But what happens when even your own body is too old or too weak to respond to what God is promising you? Abraham's answer to that was, even if your own body says there's no hope, hope anyway in God's promise. Then, you are setting yourself in position for a great move of God. Look at this passage:

> "(As it is written, I have made thee a father of many nations,) before him whom he believed, even God, who quickeneth the dead, and calleth those things which be not as though they were. Who against hope believed in hope, that he might become the father of

> many nations, according to that which was spoken, So shall thy seed be. And being not weak in faith, he considered not his own body now dead, when he was about an hundred years old, neither yet the deadness of Sarah's womb: He staggered not at the promise of God through unbelief; but was strong in faith, giving glory to God; And being fully persuaded that, what he had promised, he was able also to perform."
>
> (Romans 4:17)

Abraham was introduced to the God that brought dead things to life and called things which be not as though they were. When you are fortunate enough to connect with someone like that, all natural barriers disappear. Nothing is impossible. And, you are given an opportunity to experience something few of us have experienced, an unusual move of God.

Abraham's response to the Almighty God was to remove every obstacle and every hindrance, to prepare his entire life for what God had spoken. He would not even consider his own body, nor the body of his wife. He refused to waver in his faith. Abraham somehow sensed that this was the chance of a lifetime. In spite of considerable adversity, he gave glory to God and kept his faith strong. Finally, God had found someone who would really believe him. As a result, not only did Abraham receive a son in his old age, but he was honored by God as father of all believers (Galatians 3:29).

Would you like to do a significant work for God? Believe Him. Rearrange your life around His promises. Then the favor God gave to Abraham will come on you.

Faith That Makes God Take Notice

Dear Believer,

One man in history had the kind of faith that made even God Almighty take notice. Without any living examples in his time to pattern after, Abraham made the sole decision to believe God at all costs.

The promises God made to him seemed more suited for a young man with a fertile wife. But God promised to this elderly childless couple, descendants that could not be numbered. At the time of God's initial promise, Abraham and Sarah were 75 and 65. Twenty-five years elapsed before the promise came to pass. Anyone else would have given up and lost all hope. Not Abraham. He refused to be moved by anything, even the hopelessness displayed by his own body. He had heard from God and that was all that mattered. Please read the following passage:

> "[For Abraham, human reason for] hope being gone, hoped on in faith that he should become the father of many nations, as he had been promised, So [numberless] shall your descendants be. He did

not weaken in faith when he considered the [utter] impotence of his own body, which was as good as dead because he was about a hundred years old, or [when he considered] the barrenness of Sarah's [deadened] womb. No unbelief or distrust made him waver (doubtingly question) concerning the promise of God, but he grew strong and was empowered by faith as he gave praise and glory to God, Fully satisfied and assured that God was able and mighty to keep His word and to do what He had promised. That is why his faith was credited to him as righteousness (right standing with God)."

(Romans 4:18-22, Amplified Bible, Classic Edition)

Centuries later, after the promise had been fulfilled and Abraham had long since moved off the scene, God was still showcasing Abraham's remarkable faith. Paul recorded in the passage above that as time passed Abraham didn't grow weaker in faith, but stronger, giving praises and glory to God. That's quite a challenge! Instead of doubting or complaining, spend time praising and giving God glory. How could he praise in the face of such a depressing set of circumstances? Because he was persuaded that what God had said He would certainly do. It was cause for celebration instead of frustration. Can you believe God beyond your circumstances? If you can, God will treat you the same way He treated Abraham. He will fulfill His promise to you.

Sowing In Tears Reaping In Joy

"They that sow in tears shall reap in joy. He that goeth forth and weepeth, bearing precious seed, shall doubtless come again with rejoicing, bringing his sheaves with him."

(Psalm 126:5)

Dear Believer,

Over the years, many have found strength and comfort in this scripture. It speaks of the suffering that happens in the process of planting precious seed. <u>Precious seed is any promise from the Word of God</u>. Those of us who have sown this type of seed for a harvest are quite familiar with this experience. There are often miserable conditions prevailing at the time of planting, even to the point of sadness and tears.

Sickness and pain, poverty and debt, or confusion and upset can hang overhead like storm clouds threatening a downpour. However, no matter how forbidding conditions appear, the seed must be planted. God's Word is the only force that can make real change. The Word actually is God

(John 1:1). It is the one force that Satan knows will defeat him every time.

One thing must be remembered. Seed, no matter how potent, is ineffective until planted. It is planted when we meditate on it day and night (Joshua 1:8) or when we believe in our hearts and continually speak it out of our mouths (Mark 11:23).

Whenever we speak God's promises over our situations, we are essentially planting seeds for total change. The Bible reveals that the Word of God is seed (Mark 4:14, 1 Peter 1:23). It's power is to bring a harvest at an appointed time in the future. The future can be as soon as the next moment or as long as several years, but the harvest is certain.

Look again at the last part of the scripture above, **"He shall doubtless come again with rejoicing, bringing his sheaves with him."** There is no doubt that if you plant the Word of God, even in tears and sadness, your time of rejoicing is on its way!

I Will Never Leave You Nor Forsake You

Dear Believer,

It is often quite revealing when we examine closely what the scriptures actually say in the original Greek language. Oftentimes, there is so much more meaning when we look more closely at the original wording. For example, Hebrews 13:5 has a wonderful message as follows:

> "Let your conversation be without covetousness; and be content with such things as ye have: for he hath said, I will never leave thee, nor forsake thee."

Covetousness is an ungodly pursuit of and an unholy desire for possessions that another person has. Especially in this society, having possessions is a status symbol that is hard to ignore. Having, at least, what others have is sometimes a very real desire, whether we express it or not. It can be disguised as healthy ambition. But, letting that desire get into the forefront of your mind is a tool the enemy uses to distract us from the blessings God is always in the process of providing for each of us.

The reason God gives for being content with the things we have is because God said, "I will never leave thee." But in the Greek, it is as strong a statement as has ever been made from the lips of God. The statement is more accurately read like this in the Amplified Bible, Classic Edition:

> **"Let your character *or* moral disposition be free from love of money [including greed, avarice, lust, and craving for earthly possessions] and be satisfied with your present [circumstances and with what you have]; for He [God] Himself has said, I will not in any way fail you *nor* give you up *nor* leave you without support. [I will] not, [I will] not, [I will] not in any degree leave you helpless *nor* forsake *nor* let [you] down (relax My hold on you)! [Assuredly not!]."**
>
> (Hebrews 13:5)

Since we have such a strong statement from the Lord, we should never allow ourselves to get stressed or depressed over what someone else has. If God is our support, no good thing will be withheld (Psalm 84:11).

Let's Praise and Worship the Lord

Dear Believer,

Recently I began to feel a strong desire to spend more time in worship and praise. Maybe, like me, you thought as long as your worship was from the heart it didn't matter what form it took. With a little study on the subject, I was inspired by what I learned.

Worship is an act of our wills. The way we feel has little to do with it. One should not always expect to feel like praising and worshiping. "Just do it!" The feeling will often follow the submission to the directive to "let everything that has breath praise the Lord" (Psalm 150:6). You may not realize it but, if lately you've encountered difficult trials and tests, you **need** to praise him.

Sometimes it can be the **only way** to victory. (Please read Acts 16:22-26).

> "**And the multitude rose up together against them: and the magistrates rent off their clothes, and commanded to beat them.**

> **And when they had laid many stripes upon them, they cast them into prison, charging the jailor to keep them safely: Who, having received such a charge, thrust them into the inner prison, and made their feet fast in the stocks. And at midnight Paul and Silas prayed, and sang praises unto God: and the prisoners heard them. And suddenly there was a great earthquake, so that the foundations of the prison were shaken: and immediately all the doors were opened, and every one's bands were loosed."**
>
> (King James Version)

I recently saw a young pastor praising and leaping into the air in total disregard of the people around him. It looked as though he was determined to have a personal time with his God regardless. Everyone around him caught his sincerity and began to praise God along with him. Then the unmistakable presence of the Lord entered the room and God ministered to the needs of the people. I thought to myself, *"Lord, I'm going to begin to praise and worship with my total attention on You. As a matter of fact, from now on when I praise You, I'll shut everyone and everything out. It will always be something personal and special between You and me."*

In times of worship, indifference or apathy is just plain "dumb." When we draw near to God, He will draw near to us (James 4:8). Neglecting to worship makes you a big loser because of the blessings forfeited and supernatural opportunities missed. Don't miss your deliverance. Worship and praise the Lord.

Words That Come To Pass

Dear Believer,

Long ago, God created the world we know using the power of His spoken words. After the fall of Adam, we as a fallen race of people never imagined such power could come from anyone else. For so long it seemed fitting that God remain the only one with that amazing ability. We never seriously expected to use words the way He does.

Centuries have passed since the Lord said, "Let there be light" (Genesis 1:3). But God is now revealing to His people His intentions that our words be just as powerful as His. Apparently, man is to accomplish His divine mandate to take dominion over the earth by rediscovering the power of the spoken Word. Jesus essentially taught that you can have what you say and believe. In Mark 11:22-23 we read,

> "**And Jesus answering saith unto them, Have faith in God. For verily I say unto you, That whosoever shall say unto this mountain, Be thou removed, and be thou cast into the sea; and shall not doubt in his heart, but shall believe that those things which he**

saith shall come to pass; he shall have whatsoever he saith."

This verse, as impossible as it seems to our natural thinking, was spoken by Jesus and therefore legitimately places us in a class with our Father God. No other beings than we have any knowledge of having access to this law. Here Jesus places man's speech on the same level as that of the Father God. According to Jesus, words spoken without doubting will produce whatever is said. But to exercise this principle, we are required not only to believe in God, but surprisingly, we are admonished to **believe in the words we speak**. The disciples never heard anything like this; that they should begin to count their own words as potentially powerful.

Using words like our Heavenly Father uses them will take a real transformation in our thinking and actions. But Paul encouraged that very change when he said, **"be not conformed to this world but be ye transformed by the renewing of your mind"** (Romans 12:2).

We must now be more diligent to make this change and get accustomed to using the power our Father has provided for us.

Living on a Higher Level

"And the LORD shall make thee the head, and not the tail; and thou shalt be above only, and thou shalt not be beneath."

(Deuteronomy 28:13)

"If ye then be risen with Christ, seek those things which are above, where Christ sitteth on the right hand of God. Set your affection on things above, not on things on the earth."

(Colossians 3:1-2)

Dear Believer,

In every situation and in every trial there is a normal way to do things, which is acceptable to just about everyone, and then there's a higher way. God told Israel, "My ways are higher than your ways," (Isaiah 55:9). No matter how much we misunderstand what He's doing, everyone knows God's ways are best. Just knowing that there is a better way in God is a great comfort. Thank God we're not limited to what we know here on earth.

Last week, I began to experience some alarming flu-like symptoms, a combination of joint aches with fatigue, accompanied by uncontrollable sneezing and congestion. I kept speaking the healing scriptures over my condition. This has always worked within a short time, but this time was different. The misery lingered. Although I am rarely sick, I was happy to lie down to rest. I felt some relief as I stood on the Word, but not complete healing. My wife gave me some medication to try to check the symptoms but nothing was effective.

On the fourth night, I suddenly woke up at about 3:00AM. As I went into the bathroom, immediately God began to speak to my heart about the higher way we have of living. It is a choice we make. Others may live on the things that are seen, but we live on what the Word says. In the kingdom of God there is a higher system of healing, it's by the Word of God. God let me know that I was being healed the higher way. This had nothing to do with how I felt, but everything to do with the power of His Word. As I returned to bed, it was as if I had just received something special from the Lord. As I drifted off to dreams, I sensed my body being healed in my joints. The congestion and sneezing disappeared. I felt as if I was lying in a rich warm pool of healing. I just lay there for hours soaking in that wonderful pool. I cannot remember a time when I felt so good. It was a miracle. Halfway between sleep and dreams I began communing with God regarding certain revelations in the Word

He wanted to express. It was amazing to be healed in this manner, while at the same time communing with the Lord. God's Word never fails. If He did it for me, He'll do it for you. Don't be distracted. Stay on the high way.

Faith That Grows Stronger With Time

"Against all hope, Abraham in hope believed and so became the father of many nations, just as it had been said to him, 'So shall your offspring be.' Without weakening in his faith, he faced the fact that his body was as good as dead—since he was about a hundred years old—and that Sarah's womb was also dead. Yet he did not waver through unbelief regarding the promise of God, but was strengthened in his faith and gave glory to God, being fully persuaded that God had power to do what he had promised."

(Romans 4:18-21 New International Version)

Dear Believer,

Some of the most expensive things in life are things that improve with time. Diamonds, wines, antiques, sound investments, etc., only reach optimum value with time. Faith is in the same category. If held and nourished, it will grow ever stronger with time. But many believers haven't discovered this secret. Instead, as time elapses, they grow weaker and ultimately give up on God's promises. They don't know that time is not the enemy of faith, but the true test of its authenticity and an enhancer of its value.

Abraham's faith in God is a great example. He received a promise from God at age 75 that did not come to pass until he was 100 years old. The amazing thing is that during his waiting period, he didn't weaken, but actually <u>grew stronger</u> in faith. Instead of doubting as those precious years expired, he discovered that time could be used to strengthen his faith. How was this possible in the face of such hopelessness? Abraham was persuaded.

He knew enough about God to believe in the absolute certainty of His Word. To him, once God made a promise nothing else mattered. He knew that if he rearranged his life's priorities around what God said, he could not be denied miraculous results. Instead of yielding to the myriad of questions and doubts which must have assaulted his natural mind daily, he gave God glory. In other words, he focused on God's stellar reputation and outstanding ability. As far as he was concerned, it was a sure thing. He deliberately stopped considering any reason to doubt, like his age or how hopeless things appeared. As far as he was concerned, God had spoken and now each day that passed would only draw him ever closer to the miracle.

Can I have faith that strengthens with time? Certainly yes! Refuse the temptation to get weary as time passes. Faith doesn't tire with time. **"And let us not be weary in well doing; for in due season we shall reap, if we faint not"** (Galatians 6:9 King James Version). How can I keep from being weary in my faith? Take a page from Abraham's notes. Don't allow your body or any outward circumstance to dictate the strength of your faith. Occupy the passing time by continually giving glory to God no matter how you feel. In time, you will find yourself intimately involved in a relationship with God that is without limits.

Faith Never Grows Old

Dear Believer,

If you're not watchful, time will whittle away at your faith. By that I mean, what you started out so fervently believing God for a little while ago, if you're not careful, can all but disappear. Almost as if you never even asked God for it. It's commonly expected that as time passes some things lose their strength and their urgency. Unfortunately, we have allowed that type of thinking to sap the strength of our faith. In our youth, we have lots of energy and lots of zeal, but as time passes some of us slow down so much that we just don't "get our hopes up" anymore.

But faith, like the Word on which it depends, <u>never gets old</u>. It is always alive and powerful. As a matter of fact, God expects us to maintain our faith against the ever-present force of time erosion. A great example is that of Caleb, who believed God for the conquest of the Promised Land. He stood in faith against the majority who feared that the giants would certainly overpower them. He reported, "We are well able to overcome" (Numbers 13:30). Tragically, he and Joshua were outvoted and the people refused to enter the Land of Promise. Worse still, they angered God with their unbelief and it would be another forty years before they could return.

Remarkably, Caleb never lost faith, but maintained his stand as his generation all wasted away in the wilderness. With them gone, Caleb yet did not weaken in his faith. It's delightful to read what he said 45 years later (Joshua 14:10-14 New International Version).

> "'Now then, just as the Lord promised, he has kept me alive for forty-five years since the time he said this to Moses, while Israel moved about in the wilderness. So here I am today, eighty-five years old! I am still as strong today as the day Moses sent me out; I'm just as vigorous to go out to battle now as I was then. Now give me this hill country that the Lord promised me that day. You yourself heard then that the Anakites were there and their cities were large and fortified, but, the Lord helping me, I will drive them out just as he said.'
>
> Then Joshua blessed Caleb son of Jephunneh and gave him Hebron as his inheritance. So Hebron has belonged to Caleb son of Jephunneh the Kenizzite ever since, because he followed the Lord, the God of Israel, wholeheartedly."
>
> (Joshua 14:10-14 New International Version)

Surprisingly, this is the statement of an unsaved man of the Old Covenant who refused to let his faith get weak no matter how long it took. What is your excuse? Let's get busy and rekindle our faith fire. Go back and get the requests you had long ago. Write them down and bring them again before the Lord. Nothing is impossible! Nothing!

Basics for Strong Faith

"Let us therefore fear, lest, a promise being left us of entering into his rest, any of you should seem to come short of it. For unto us was the gospel preached, as well as unto them: but the word preached did not profit them, not being mixed with faith in them that heard it."

(Hebrews 4:1-2 King James Version)

Dear Believer,

Throughout the Bible, one major point is emphasized. Without faith, we cannot expect to receive anything that is promised from the Lord. Actually, without it, it's impossible to please Him. It just makes sense that if that is what it takes to please God, we must make it our priority to get it and keep it active in our lives.

Faith is the spiritual force designed by God for every believer to use at all times to access the invisible unlimited bounty of Heaven and to bring it into the visible realm of earth. It is the force God Himself used to create the universe in which we live (Hebrews 11:3). Jesus said any believer can use even a little of it to move mountains and to do impossible feats (Matthew 17:20). It is truly an amazing power that can overcome anything in this world (1 John 5:4). And, to our utter delight, this amazing force called faith is designed to be our servant (Luke 17:7). With such awesome power within our reach, why is it some Christians yet have a difficult time believing for healing or finances or miracles? They have some faith but it's very weak. It's what Jesus called "little faith" or short-term faith.

We need the kind of faith that gets stronger, not weaker, with time. How can we obtain it?

Here are some basics for strong faith. 1. **Faith comes by hearing the Word repeatedly.** (Romans 10:17) Daily meditation and memorization of the Word accomplishes this. 2. **Faith works by love.** (Galatians 5:6) This is accomplished by keeping ourselves under the commandment of love at all times. 3. **Faith is released out of a believing heart through spoken words and corresponding actions.** (Mark 11:22-24, James 2:26) Speaking the Word over our circumstances, no matter how severe they are, and acting like the Word is true, no matter what we see, will put the force of faith to work for us in every situation. 4. **Stay in expectancy.** Don't allow yourself to get weary. Give glory to God until you see the manifestation. (Galatians 6:9)

Your Faith is Waiting to Serve You

Dear Believer,

Some of us in our youth dreamed of being wealthy enough to have servants answering at our every beck and call. For most of us, it has been more dream than reality. But what would you say if you discovered that at this moment there is a servant eagerly waiting to serve you? <u>Your faith is designed by God to be your servant.</u> It is designed to accomplish whatever you desire and believe. It is a servant that never tires of bringing into being what we believe.

In the passage below, the followers of Jesus asked Him to increase their faith. He first spoke of faith as a grain of mustard seed. But then, surprisingly, He connected His teaching on faith to the experience of having a servant. This was something everyone in that culture understood very well. They all knew that a servant typically worked in the field and did whatever else was ordered by his master. Can you see that your faith is your servant? It must not only be sent to get your daily provisions, but also to get results in every other area of your life.

"The apostles said to the Lord, 'Increase our faith!' He replied, 'If you have faith as small as a mustard seed, you can say to this mulberry tree, 'Be uprooted and planted in the sea,' and it will obey you. 'Suppose one of you has a servant plowing or looking after the sheep. Will he say to the servant when he comes in from the field, 'Come along now and sit down to eat'? Won't he rather say, 'Prepare my supper, get yourself ready and wait on me while I eat and drink; after that you may eat and drink?'"

(Luke 17:5-8)

Send your faith to get your healing, then your money. Don't let it rest. Faith never tires. But be wise. Feed it well on the Word of God daily. Then release it through words and actions everyday to accomplish the challenging chores of this life. In time, you'll be able to witness the fact that your faith conquers anything this world sends your way (1 John 5:4).

Top Ten Reasons to Believe

Dear Believer,

The late night talk show host, David Letterman, for years poked fun at just about everything through his "Top Ten Reasons" comedy routine. The segment is a spoof of scientific polls, which so many now rely on to find out what various people in the country are thinking. Starting with number ten and ending with supposedly the most popular reason, each one is an increasingly comical statement, which drives home the point of the farce.

The humor is in the fact that the poll is neither scientific nor a real poll at all. It is concocted completely by comedy writers.

We have been given many reasons to doubt the Word of God in this society. Our enemy stops at nothing to bring up even the silliest reasons to doubt. But to think that he can win at any time against God is ludicrous. I thought it would be good to give the top ten reasons for your faith to grow stronger. Instead of fretting with doubts, this is a good exercise to use to laugh at the lies of the devil. In descending order here they are:

TOP TEN REASONS FOR YOUR FAITH TO GROW STRONGER

10. Heaven and earth will pass away before God's Word fails. (Matthew 24:35)

9. Faith will defeat anything the world brings against you. (1 John 5:4)

8. Jesus said, if you believe nothing is impossible. (Matthew 17:20)

7. Everything we need has already been released to us by our Father. (2 Peter 1:3)

6. Things that you can see are only temporary and subject to change. (2 Corinthians 4:18)

5. Every day that passes brings us closer to the fulfillment of God's promise. (Hebrews 6:12)

4. If we don't doubt, we will have whatever we say. (Mark 11:23)

3. Just like our Father, our words of faith never return to us void. (Isaiah 55:11, Matthew 11:23)

2. Faith is my servant, accomplishing everything I need in this life. (Luke 17:6,7)

1. Living by faith pleases our God. (Hebrews 11:6)

Now take some time and laugh at the lies of Devil. He is forever defeated.

Remember What He Said to You

"Therefore we ought to give the more earnest heed to the things which we have heard, lest at any time we should let them slip."

(Hebrews 2:1)

Dear Believer,

If you are a person who talks to the Lord you know that you need to keep a pen and pad handy to catch the many statements your Father makes during your time together. God's words are never just "small talk." When He speaks, He often says things that we need to keep in mind as the week unfolds. His words can keep us from danger and protect us in the middle of conflict. Just one word or statement from the Lord can mean the difference between disaster and victory. Like an anchor, His words keep us steady during stormy times.

The problem is that as each new morning arrives, we have a tendency to forget what God said to us yesterday. That's a costly mistake. Because He loves us, God is always looking out for us. He knows what's ahead.

Whenever He speaks, if we will listen, we'll be able to get into a position of advantage. Coming events cannot take us by surprise or catch us unprepared when we remember the little statements He spoke just a little while ago.

Take time today to remember the things the Lord spoke to you. In His simple statements you will find both peace and power for whatever you will face. God's words are always worth remembering. After all, if His followers had not written the things He said to them, we would not have the Bible today.

Blessed With Every Spiritual Blessing

> "Praise be to the God and Father of our Lord Jesus Christ, who has blessed us in the heavenly realms with every spiritual blessing in Christ."
>
> (Ephesians 1:3 New International Version)

Dear Believer,

As believers, we have so much for which to be thankful. Life, health and strength are what my parents always thanked God for and admonished us to do likewise. To this day, I consider these to be valuable blessings that people take for granted. But as I learn more about the Lord, I have encountered a category of blessing that many Christians simply have no idea we have received.

In Christ, we have been given every spiritual blessing, every one of them. Nothing is held back. This is truly an astounding endowment. The spiritual realm has always ruled the natural physical realm, and a blessing has always been the empowerment to prosper. If God has given to us <u>every spiritual empowerment to prosper</u>, we have been given the keys to the kingdom. Please take some time and think about what it means to actually possess <u>every spiritual blessing</u>.

From time to time, I have been generously blessed by people who gave out of their wealth. But no wealthy benefactor has ever considered sharing with me everything he/she owns. Yet Paul reveals to us that we have already been blessed (empowered) by our Father with <u>every</u> spiritual blessing (empowerment). To the unlearned, "spiritual" means unseen and imaginary. But to the enlightened, it is the very kingdom of God himself which can create in the earth whatever it desires and believes.

No doubt, it will take us some time to realize the magnitude of this blessing. It's off the scale! But let's just receive it by faith right now and praise God continually for it.

Everyone who Asks Receives (Matt. 7:8)

Dear Believer,

We have heard this passage of scripture for years. It's a comforting verse with open-ended promises. It promises that if you expend the effort to ask, seek and knock, and don't give up, you will be rewarded. But do you see the very next statement Jesus makes? He said, "Everyone who asks receives" (New International Version). The whole world should rejoice over this statement. But that's not the typical response. Because for most of us, that has not been our experience! There are many things over the years that we asked for that just never materialized.

Did Jesus briefly lose touch with reality or is there something we need to learn? I think you'll agree that there's something more we need to learn. "Asking," in line with the scripture, was never meant to end with disappointment or lack. It is designed by God to end in receiving and in "full joy." Jesus boldly said, "Ask, and ye shall receive, that your joy may be full" (John 16:24 King James Version). How did we get so far away from His intentions?

To address this question, we must first clear up a misconception that continues to wreak havoc in the Body of Christ. God is not to blame for the many misfortunes that we encounter. You need to know that if you pray asking for patience, God will not give you cancer. Furthermore, He will not take the lives of your children or loved ones in response to your request for more love. Your enemy, Satan, comes to steal, to kill and to destroy (Please read John 10:10). Jesus tried to clear this up when he said:

> "Which of you, if his son asks for bread, will give him a stone? Or if he asks for a fish, will give him a snake? If you, then, though you are evil, know how to give good gifts to your children, how much more will your Father in heaven give good gifts to those who ask him!"
>
> (Matthew 7:9-11 New International Version)

God is ready to give good gifts.

Receiving is Automatic

Dear Believer,

In our walk with the Lord, there is much for us to learn about seemingly simple things. One of those simple things is "asking." Jesus declared that everyone who asks also receives. It is surprising that he said, "EVERYONE!" Apparently, God designed "receiving" to be automatic every time "asking" is done, according to the scriptures. Can you believe that everyone who asks receives? Listen carefully to the words of Jesus:

> "Until now you have not asked for anything in my name. Ask and you will receive, and your joy will be complete."
>
> (John 16:24)

> "Therefore I tell you, whatever you ask for in prayer, believe that you have received it, and it will be yours."
>
> (Mark 11:24)

In order for this principle to work, after we ask, we cannot ever leave out believing that <u>we have received</u>. EVERYONE WHO ASKS RECEIVES. Although Jesus was very aware that many of His listeners had failed for years to receive from God, this spiritual law needed to be unveiled. This powerful law, if followed, will produce every time and for anyone. But if ignored or violated, it will simply not work.

Here's the same principle repeated by John some years later;

> **"This is the confidence we have in approaching God: that if we ask anything according to his will, he hears us. And if we know that he hears us—whatever we ask—we know that we have what we asked of him."**
>
> (1 John 5:14-15)

According to John, if we have asked in line with His Word, the Lord hears us and that qualifies us for receiving. John declared, "WE KNOW THAT WE HAVE WHAT WE ASKED." Confidence is critical whenever we ask. It qualifies "asking" to automatically become "receiving."

Advanced Provisions

Dear Believer,

Years ago when I was child, my parents taught me that whenever I wanted something from them, there was a proper way of asking. I was instructed to say, "please," and immediately follow that with, "Thank You" after I received. A sure way to be scolded or "worse" was to disobey their instructions or throw a temper tantrum. Even if I was angry and impatient, I had to follow their instructions or I would not receive what I wanted. God is our Father and He has also given to us similar instructions, with an interesting difference.

From the beginning, God has always provided for man an abundance of the things he needed. This was before man was created and before he asked. It was a truly wonderful act of love and caring. It is also beyond anything we ever dreamed. But through the years, God has not gotten much acknowledgment for it. Nevertheless, His established pattern was to continue to anticipate everything we would ever need and, ahead of our arrival, place all of it within our reach. Look at these scriptures:

> "His divine power has given us everything we need for life and godliness through our knowledge of Him."
>
> (2 Peter 1:3)

> "You made us a little lower than you yourself, and you have crowned us with glory and honor. You let us rule everything your hands have made. And you put all of it under our power—the sheep and the cattle, and every wild animal, the birds in the sky, the fish in the sea, and all ocean creatures."
>
> (Psalm 8:5-8 Contemporary English Version)

Far in advance, God has always provided for you. His "works were finished from the foundation of the world" (Hebrews 4:3 King James Version). To every person on earth, God offers this abundance. But only those who believe and act will tap into that provision. We honor God when we ask properly by <u>believing we receive when we ask</u> (Mark 11:24). This act of faith gives God honor. It finally acknowledges the great love he displayed by supernaturally providing for us before we ever existed.

Rising Above the Clouds

Dear Believer,

I realize that for some of us there is no real alternative to believing the promises of God. But in this society we have become accustomed to options. We can vote Democratic or Republican. We can choose to "take out" or sit down for dinner. We can decide to lease or own our automobiles. Even when we live for God, there are yet several ways to get results. But some are much more powerful than others. Isaiah wrote:

> **"For my thoughts are not your thoughts, neither are your ways my ways, saith the LORD. For as the heavens are higher than the earth, so are my ways higher than your ways, and my thoughts than your thoughts."**
>
> (Isaiah 55:8,9)

Before us are always at least two choices, our ways and His ways. But He also said His ways are <u>higher</u>. To me, that means better or higher in value and priority, higher in authority and power as well. Anyone who has flown in a plane knows that when the plane breaks through the clouds, the sun is always shining. Dark clouds and rain are not a factor the higher you fly. So it is with the Word of God. It is the highest way of accomplishing results.

Some effort is required to maintain the altitude needed to walk in the Word of God. But it's well worth any energy and time required.

Praises be to God who has permanently raised every believer to experience the higher ways of God. Paul said, **"And hath raised us up together, and made us sit together in heavenly places in Christ Jesus"** (Ephesians 2:6).

How do we experience the higher ways of God? We can rise above the clouds as we surround ourselves with His words. The sun shines brightly as we speak them out of our mouths and keep them in our hearts all day long. When the pressure comes, we ascend by His words far above every dark cloud of the enemy.

Reconciled

Dear Believer,

Are you familiar with the verse that starts out like this, **"if any man be in Christ Jesus, he is a new creature…"**? This is the new creation verse for all believers. Through it, we know that in our lives, **"old things have passed away and all things are become new"** (2 Corinthians 5:17). But don't overlook the supernatural restoration that happened for us all in the next verse.

> **"But all things are from God, Who through Jesus Christ reconciled us to Himself [received us into favor, brought us into harmony with Himself]."**
>
> (2 Corinthians 5:18 Amplified Bible Classic Edition)

The prospect of being "reconciled" to God is quite exciting. It implies that we were together at one time. We had a "falling out" and separated. But the reason for our separation has been resolved, and we have reunited. Now and forever, we both agree that we belong together. This coincides perfectly with Bible history. In the beginning, we were together with God.

Because of sin, we separated. Now through Jesus, we have reunited to a relationship in which nothing shall separate us and all things work together for our good.

That would mean that our new relationship with God is like Adam and Eve's before the fall. We can now enjoy being reconciled, which means "received into favor and brought into harmony with God." Favor and harmony with God is nothing short of Heaven on earth.

Disarm the Enemy

Dear Believer,

It is something to behold how much effort the enemy puts into attacking our confidence in God's Word. He launches a constant barrage of adversities aimed at derailing our trust in the Word. His intended purpose is to cause uncertainty regarding what God has said. This has been an effective strategy since the Garden of Eden. Since it worked so well then, and with such devastating consequences for mankind, it is Satan's weapon of choice. As a result, any unsuspecting believer is in for battle after battle when uncertainty creeps in.

Confidence in the Word of our God is essential to our very existence. We believe that the entire world in which we live was formed by the Word (Hebrews 11:3). The victorious faith by which we can overcome anything the world brings against us, relies on it (1 John 5:4). And, John 1:1 tells us that the Word actually is, in essence, the Almighty God. Jesus said if we believe "nothing is impossible" (Matthew 17:20 King James Version). The only hope our enemy has of defeating us is in causing uncertainty about the integrity of the Word.

Let's disarm him right now. Refuse to listen to the lies of the Devil. Wipe the picture of hopelessness from your imagination. Replace every thought of defeat with the promises of God. Paul said be transformed by renewing your mind (Romans 12:2). Do this until you sense a transformation taking place, until you begin to respond to the pressures of your circumstances with confidence. The scriptures declare with certainty, **"Heaven and earth shall pass away, but my words shall not pass away"** (Matthew 24:35).

It's Your Unbelief!

Dear Believer,

Like you, I feel so blessed to know that faith comes by hearing and hearing the Word of God (Romans 10:17). As a result, I have turned the faith faucet on by reading the Word, listening to CD's, and speaking it daily. I can now believe God for things I could only dream of before. I envision my faith growing by the truckload. We must remember, however, that although Jesus encouraged His disciples to believe, He never spoke of them needing any more than a small amount of pure faith, even in the hardest cases (Matthew 17:20).

Remember the time the disciples returned to Jesus with a case they could not cure (Matthew 17:14-21). It was a demon-possessed boy who was tormented by a lunatic spirit. When asked why they failed to get results, Jesus did not instruct them to increase their faith. Only a small amount of faith was needed here. The problem was their unbelief. It was being allowed to contaminate their faith. The father of the demon-possessed boy said "I believe; help my unbelief" (Mark 9:24 English Standard Version). In other words, he said I have faith, but unbelief is polluting my faith.

Recently, loads of spinach were found to be contaminated with E.coli bacteria. The solution was not to increase the amount of spinach sold, but to find the source of the contamination and stop it. Faith is powerful. But in this society, saturated with fear and doubt, faith is easily contaminated.

Doubt and fear make God a liar, but faith believes He's the truth. They cannot coexist. Jesus said, "It's your unbelief." Whenever it is allowed to linger, it pollutes faith. That's when it seems you need a truckload to get results. In reality, you just need a small amount of pure simple faith.

Jesus told Jairus, after he was devastated at the news that his little girl had died, "Be not afraid, only believe" (Mark 5:36 King James Version). Don't allow fear or doubt to contaminate your pure faith. Keep it pure all day. Only believe.

Impossible

Dear Believer,

The word "impossible" always raises "red flags" with us believers. It usually represents serious obstacles to something we desire. But instead of having a discouraging effect, things that are impossible affect believers just the opposite. Like waving a red flag in front of a bull, it fires our resolve and spurs us into charging on against seemingly insurmountable odds. Since the day Jesus came back from the grave, believers have been inclined to take on the challenge of things that seem impossible.

On the flip side, however, there are some impossible things that are actually working in our favor. I'm referring to the fact that it is impossible for God to lie (Hebrews 6:8). We all celebrate the impossibility of His Word ever returning empty or "void." Another is the fact that without faith it is impossible to please God (Hebrews 11:6). This is a wonderful insight that can be used by anyone anywhere to access the things of God. There is another that came recently by a revelation shared with me. A childhood friend of mine,

Evan. E. H. Godfrey, was meditating on Mark 11:23, taking it slowly, one segment at a time to glean full meaning like this:

> "**For verily I say unto you,** (Pause) **That whosoever shall say unto this mountain, Be thou removed, and be thou cast into the sea;** (Pause) **and shall not doubt in his heart,** (Pause) **but shall believe that those things which he saith shall come to pass;** (Pause) **he shall have whatsoever he saith.**"

As he was meditating, the Lord spoke to him and said, **"It's impossible! It's impossible! If you follow this principle and line these things up. It's impossible for something <u>not</u> to happen!"**

Join with me to welcome this impossibility. When we line up with what Jesus said in this scripture, It's impossible! It's impossible! It's impossible for something not to happen!

Hallelujah!

The Greatest Proof of All

"In the beginning was the Word, and the Word was with God, and the Word was God. The same was in the beginning with God. All things were made by him; and without him was not any thing made that was made. And the Word was made flesh, and dwelt among us, (and we beheld his glory, the glory as of the only begotten of the Father,) full of grace and truth."

(John 1:1-3;14)

Dear Believer,

The greatest proof of the power of the Word in history is the birth of Jesus. After centuries of speaking of His birth, from the time of Moses to the prophets of old, expectations were high in the hearts and minds of the people. The word of His coming was sowed time and time again, like seed into the earth, hundreds of years before His arrival. But at the appointed time, like a long awaited harvest, that Word was made flesh. Jesus was born in Bethlehem.

This was an astounding miracle for several reasons. First, the woman who birthed Him was a virgin. Secondly, although it was prophesied the child would be born in Bethlehem, Mary and Joseph lived far away in Nazareth. Thirdly, a jealous evil king did everything in his power to find and kill this child, even to the point of slaughtering every newborn child in that region.

This should fortify every believer with power to withstand the enemy's vicious attacks. If the Word in the form of a newborn baby overcame every obstacle then, it can surely overcome every adversity now. Jesus not only was born in the middle of impossible circumstances, but throughout His life, He conquered every conceivable threat known to mankind. Even when He died, death could not hold Him. This is the Word we believe in.

Be encouraged, the promises of God may seem as weak as a little baby, but don't allow yourself to be swayed. **"Whatever is born of God overcomes the world. This is the victory that overcomes the word, even our faith"** (1 John 5:4).

Don't Take "No" for an Answer

> "For the Son of God, Jesus Christ, who was preached among you by me and Silas and Timothy, was not 'Yes' and 'No,' but in him it has always been 'Yes.' For no matter how many promises God has made, they are 'Yes' in Christ. And so through him the 'Amen' is spoken by us to the glory of God."
>
> (2 Corinthians 1:19-20 New International Version)

Dear Believer,

One of the most awesome benefits of being a believer is the fact that all the promises of God come with the answer "Yes" intact. Therefore, whoever pursues His promises should not accept "No" as an answer. This provides such a solid rock for our faith to stand firm. But did you know that there were some individuals in the Bible who had little or no understanding of God's promises, but received from Him anyway, because they refused to be denied? Here is one example:

A Canaanite woman came begging Jesus to cure her daughter who was being tormented by a devil. Jesus didn't even answer her. She then pleaded with the disciples for help. They wanted to send her away, but she persisted. Finally, Jesus spoke harshly to her saying, "It's not right for me to give the children's bread to dogs." In other words, He was saying, "You know that you live like a dog. It's neither your time to receive, nor your blessing." But amazingly, she did not allow this to stop her. Refusing to be distracted or offended, she said, "Truth Lord: yet the dogs eat the crumbs which fall from their master's table." Jesus said to her, "O woman great is your faith. Be it unto thee even as thou wilt" (See Matthew 15:21-28 King James Version).

What made Jesus divert from His assignment and bless someone who was obviously a rank sinner? The power of persistence. When pursuing God's promises never allow roadblocks, setbacks or hindrances to stop you. Keep going. Keep believing. Keep speaking God's Word over your circumstances. "No" is the wrong answer.

Who Can I Count On?

Dear Believer,

In times of trouble, leaders cannot always count on receiving support and encouragement from those they lead. Too often there is none. But that's not all bad. Leadership is often lonely and sometimes it demands periods of isolation. Such sacrifices seem to be necessary prerequisites to do great things for God. Leadership costs, but it also has its rewards. It pays big dividends with God.

There are real challenges that face anyone one who makes decisions affecting others. When those decisions end in prosperity and success everyone celebrates. But when they bring unwanted or painful outcomes, loyalties can quickly fade and commitments can immediately dissolve. Here is a survival key for every leader. In painful predicaments, there is one person you should count on to encourage you to believe God. One person who knows what God has done and how many times He saved you. That person is you.

Prior to becoming king of Israel, David and his army returned home to Ziklag to experience total devastation.

While they were away, the Amalekites invaded their village, burned it to the ground and took their wives and children captive. Shocked and grieved, each soldier wept for his family until he could cry no more. The possibility that they would ever see them again faded into utter hopelessness. So deep was their anguish, they spoke of stoning their beloved leader, David. At this low point, the scripture records a desperate but determined action that David took. It states, **"but David encouraged himself in the Lord his God"** (1 Samuel 30:6). Apparently, this was just what God needed to turn this great tragedy into a great triumph. With God guiding his every move, David's army overtook the Amalekites, recovered all they lost and plundered all that the enemy had accumulated.

Is there no one around who supports you? No one to encourage you? Don't be sad; be determined. Encourage yourself. David wrote, **"Why, my soul, are you downcast? Why so disturbed within me? Put your hope in God, for I will yet praise him, my Savior and my God"** (Psalm 42:11 New International Version).

Temporary Setbacks

"Sing, barren woman, you who never bore a child; burst into song, shout for joy, you who were never in labor."

(Isaiah 54:1)

Dear Believer,

To be in lack while others are enjoying plenty is hard. Similarly, to remain childless while all around you everyone else is being blessed with children can be a bitter pill. Although some believers give and live just as righteously as others, for some reason, their season of blessing is on hold. Try as they may, their breakthrough is delayed. To be "barren" is a harsh reality both in the spiritual and in the natural. Any individual who keeps trying and failing, male or female, is bound to begin to feel forsaken. But, one thing God promised He would never do to His people, is forsake them (Hebrews 13:5).

In Israel, God promised that there would not be any barren in the land if they kept His commandments. Fertility was part of the covenant. To be barren, therefore, was a curse that carried a stigma. But we find some notable women who bore this stigma, yet prospered. Among them was Abraham's wife, Sarah; Hannah, the mother of the prophet Samuel; and Elizabeth, the mother of John the Baptist. In each of these women, prolonged hardship was merely a prelude to a tremendous move of God. Nowadays we realize that being barren is never permanent but only a temporary setback. It is more accurately described as <u>blessings delayed but not denied</u>.

God has prescribed a peculiar exercise for the barren. He said, "Sing," "Burst into song" and "Shout for joy." If you are barren, that's the last thing you feel like doing. But God goes even further to say, "Enlarge your tent, stretch your curtains, lengthen your cords and strengthen your stakes" (Isaiah 54:2). In other words, don't spend any time in self-pity. Make plans and set goals. Spend your time preparing for the blessings God promised you. You are not forgotten and you will not be left out. From ancient times He promised, **"Thou shall be blessed above all people: there shall not be male or female barren among you"** (Deuteronomy 7:14 King James Version).

Fire the Big Guns

"Let the saints be joyful in glory: let them sing aloud upon their beds. Let the high praises of God be in their mouth, and a twoedged sword in their hand; to execute vengeance upon the heathen."

(Psalm 149:5-6)

Dear Believer,

When there is no way out and no visible means of rescue, believers have access to overwhelming force that will turn the tide every time. Like no other weapon in the Christian arsenal, singing and praising God is like firing big guns, especially in hopeless situations. Look at the following incidents:

King Jehoshaphat faced a fearsome enemy made up of the armies of three countries. In desperation, he and all of Israel fasted and sought the Lord. He received from the Lord the message, "The battle is not yours, but God's" (2 Chronicles 20:15). On the morning of the battle, he did a very odd thing. He placed singers in the front of his army. They went before the army to the battle singing and praising God. In response to this, God himself ambushed the enemy. The invading armies became so confused; they actually fought and destroyed each other. Their complete annihilation came from singing and praising.

In Acts 16:16-28, most of us have read about Paul and Silas' ordeal. Having cast a spirit out of a little girl, they were hauled before the town judges and convicted of breaking the law. The punishment was that they be publicly stripped and lashed with many stripes. After a severe beating, they were thrown into an inner cell of the jail and their feet fastened in stocks.

But at midnight they did something quite abnormal and unexpected. Paul and Silas prayed and sang praises unto God so loudly the other prisoners heard them. Suddenly, a violent earthquake hit the place and everyone's chains came loose. This is real-life example of the power we release upon our enemies in simple songs and praises.

Do you want to rout the enemy at the very moment he's about to celebrate your defeat? Do the unexpected. Sing and praise. When it looks and feels the worst, sing songs and praise. In so doing, you fire big guns which wreak havoc in the enemy's camp.

Just Keep Going

Dear Believer,

What David accomplished at Ziklag should go down in history as one of the most inspiring feats of faith of all time. Imagine yourself the leader of 600 weary men who have been walking for three days, only to arrive home and find it burned to the ground. Your loved ones are missing and presumed dead. You know within that you were anointed by God to be king, but now there is very little evidence of that. Your men have followed you through many hardships, living in caves, sleeping in open fields, and being chased by thousands of soldiers. Now those men are tired and bitter and they want to stone you. The scriptures record that David encouraged himself in the Lord, but that was not enough. He would now have to find strength beyond any effort he had ever displayed just to keep going.

The Lord told David to pursue, that he would definitely overtake his enemy and recover all. This would have been a challenge even with fresh troops. But the enemy had at least a three day head start. So the task ahead was to march with 600 tired disheartened men fast enough to overtake them.

David set out not even knowing where his enemy was. Another setback hit when 200 of his men became so exhausted they gave up and stayed behind. Undeterred, David kept going with a third less army. But as they pressed onward, they found a slave who had fallen sick that the enemy had left behind. He led them right to the camp of the Amelakites. At that point, David's men faced an untold number spread out over the countryside, rejoicing and celebrating over the spoil they had taken. The Bible records that David led his men into the camp and slaughtered them all that night to the evening of the next day. Not one escaped, except the young men riding camels.

Just as in the time of David, you may be called upon to keep going in the face of continuing setbacks. Don't be fooled by the tenacity of the enemy. In God, victory is always yours. How bad do you want it? Take on God's strength and keep going. Your God "gives power to the faint and to them that have no might he increases strength" (Isaiah 40:29 English Standard Version).

"Lord, Make Him Pay"

Dear Believer,

The enemy has done tremendous damage in our lives and the lives of our loved ones for years now. He has managed to bring about every misery known to our world to afflict us. Families have been torn apart, lives have been permanently ruined and poverty has plagued thousands. We are often so glad to be delivered from his clutches that we just want to be saved and get on with our lives. But there's something that's being missed here. Vengeance!

Don't misunderstand me. I know that the Lord said that vengeance is His. That's the very reason for this writing. It's time for God to take vengeance upon His enemies. But He needs our cooperation. Proverbs 6:30-31 states, **"Men do not despise a thief, if he steal to satisfy his soul when he is hungry; But if he be found, he shall restore sevenfold; he shall give all the substance of his house"** (New International Version).

A thief must pay sevenfold according to this verse of scripture. According to Jesus, our enemy is a known thief (John

10:10). Another verse, Deuteronomy 28:7 states, **"The LORD will grant that the enemies who rise up against you will be defeated before you. They will come at you from one direction but flee from you in seven"** (New International Version). The number seven is again stated in this list of promised blessings for the people of God. The enemy will flee seven ways.

Anyone who has walked with God knows that no promise automatically comes. Believers have to speak them and believe for promises to manifest. Above is a promise concerning our enemy. I believe that we've been letting him off too easy. It's time to ask God to make him pay. Everything that is rightfully yours, from abundant finances to divine health has been stolen by the Devil. It's time to see the manifestation of vengeance upon the enemy. Let's keep a vigil, asking the Lord in this season to execute His vengeance upon our enemy. Don't let him off. It's time for him to pay for all the damage he's done.

Conceive the Image

"I had fainted, unless I had believed to see the goodness of the LORD in the land of the living."
(Psalm 27:13)

Dear Believer,

Too many believers are missing the benefits of faith because of omitting a very important part; the part of conceiving the image on the inside before we speak. Believing that you receive is "seeing" on the inside what you desire from the Lord. Conceiving an image is almost like becoming pregnant with what we ask.

After hearing the words of Jesus about speaking to move mountains, each of us wanted to experience it. However, upon speaking to our mountainous circumstances we found that, far too often, there was no reaction. This may be partly due to the fact that we haven't taken time to conceive on the inside of us the image of what we desire.

Words bring pictures, images of what the speaker is saying. If he's speaking of a sunny day in an open field crowded with spectators watching brightly colored hot air balloons; we get the picture even though we're not physically there. Likewise, when we read God's Word, we see heavenly pictures of healing, abundance and victory. God speaks powerful heavenly pictures while we are surrounded by contradictory circumstances. He says with His stripes we are healed, while the disease is advancing and the pain is throbbing. If we can grasp His powerful words and keep His powerful pictures on the inside of us, what's inside will manifest.

So next time you get ready to speak in faith, take time beforehand to conceive the image. Feed on God's promises until what's on the inside becomes more real than what's on the outside.

It's Not What It Appears to Be

"We live by faith, not by sight."
                    (2 Corinthians 5:7 New International Version)

Dear Believer,

We are keenly aware of the difference between the way God sees things and the way we see those same things. When we're feeling sick, He says we're healed. When we're experiencing utter defeat, He says we already have the victory. When we feel weak, He tells us to say we are strong. But the real truth about it is, if we don't see things the way God sees them, we are not just misinformed; actually, we are deceived.

Much of what we view as defeat is not. It is actually deceit. The way things appear is often a deception to be overcome when we're exercising our faith in the Word of God. Believers are instructed not to walk by the way things appear, but by what we believe (2 Corinthians 4:16-18). For so long, we were educated to live within the boundaries of the physical realm. And rightly so, since that's the only world many people know. But those of us who were born again of the Spirit have rediscovered our original home. It is the realm of the spirit. The place where God lives and from which we have our origin. This is the realm from which the Word of God rules. From this vantage point, it is wonderful to know we can change the physical realm.

The entire physical world was created by the spiritual through God's words. The spirit realm is the mother of the natural world and not vice versa. Dire physical circumstances and life-threatening natural events can dictate the actions of most people, but not believers. If we believe His words (which are spiritual forces), nothing is impossible (Matthew 17:20). So, strip away the deception and reach for God's promises. Look beyond what is seen and focus on the unseen realm of God's promises and take your stand.

Look Through the Eyes of God

Dear Believer,

If we're not careful, life can really beat us down. Mistakes and failures can become a tool in the enemy's hand to ruin your day. Like storm clouds looming overhead, a downpour of condemnation is imminent if we don't take quick action. We must hurry up and get a view through the eyes of God.

What God sees is such a glorious and loving view of each of us. The way He sees us is so far superior to what we see. Let's hurry up and exchange ours for His. And since He's God, His account is much more accurate. Don't you think? Let's see through His eyes by reading what He said.

1. You are redeemed. You are valuable. (Colossians 1:14)

2. You are raised up and seated with Jesus. You have great authority in the earth. (Ephesians 2:6, John 14:13-14)

3. You are a new creature, a new species in the earth. (2 Corinthians 5:17)

4. You are reconciled and have returned to favor with God Almighty. (2 Corinthians 5:18)

5. You are the righteousness of God. You are in right standing with God. (2 Corinthians 5:21)

6. The Greater One (the Holy Spirit) lives and operates inside of you (1 John 4:4)

7. You are sons and daughters in God's very own family. (1 John 3:1,2)

This is what God sees in us. It's already written and the Devil can't do a thing about it. Rejoice! What He sees is what you really are.

Jesus Recovered All

> "For if because of one man's trespass (lapse, offense) death reigned through that one, much more surely will those who receive [God's] overflowing grace (unmerited favor) and the free gift of righteousness reign [putting them into right standing with Himself] as kings in life through the one Man Jesus Christ (the Messiah, the Anointed One)."
>
> (Romans 5:17 Amplified Bible, Classic Edition)

Dear Believer,

We all know by now that it was Adam's fatal fall that plunged our world into sin. He opened the door to death and every misery known to mankind, including sickness, poverty and defeat. But we also know that Jesus thoroughly cleaned up Adam's mess. <u>Adam lost it all, but Jesus recovered all that was lost in the fall.</u> Jesus recovered all! He purchased for each of us precious favor and right standing with God. The scripture above states, we are now to reign as kings in life. Is that the way you're living, like a king reigning in this life?

It may be somewhat surprising to realize that being chosen by God to rule as a king seldom means that ruling is automatic. Just read about Joseph, David or Solomon. There's always a jealous adversary who wants your position and who has the audacity to stake a "bogus" claim. Your enemy knows that it would indeed be a coup if he can prevent you from exercising your authority. But take heart, he is also aware that God Almighty is the one backing you up. You must, however, begin to act like God's anointed in order for His backing to manifest. Acting on His Word activates the power. If you hesitate or back down, your enemy will be emboldened. God wants to treat you like David and "prepare a table [for] you in the [very] presence of your enemies" (Psalm 23:5 King James Version).

God has already sacrificed Jesus so that you could reign as a king. Set your mind and heart on reigning in this life. Let your life conform to this part of God's will just as you would His commandments. Speak with authority, pray with power and take your place!

www.ingramcontent.com/pod-product-compliance
Lightning Source LLC
Chambersburg PA
CBHW030435010526
44118CB00011B/648